PRAISE FOR *My Man in Antibes*

"Graham Greene, top British novelist of the twentieth century, his writing by turns (and often all at once) political, romantic, thrilling, satiric, curt, hilarious, his life full of old-school adventure, possibly even espionage, plenty of danger in any case: what more fascinating friend could a person have? And what better chronicler than Graham Greene's friend Michael Mewshaw, eager young novelist in the orbit of the master, more and more trusted as time went on, closer than almost anyone got."

—BILL ROORBACH, author of
Lucky Turtle

"Michael Mewshaw, an award-winning novelist, has already chronicled his fascinating friendships with Gore Vidal and Pat Conroy. Here he combines and contrasts the remarkable story of his deprived upbringing with that of an older and already established Catholic writer: Graham Greene."

—MIRANDA SEYMOUR, author of
I Used to Live Here Once: The Haunted Life of Jean Rhys

"In a prose at times as vivid and dramatic as that of its subject, and with a comparably economical sense of place, Mewshaw's memoir offers valuable lessons about the limits of the life Greene chose to lead, a life he himself has long admired and emulated."

—ZACHARY LEADER, author of
The Life of Saul Bellow: Love and Strife, 1965-2005

MY MAN IN ANTIBES

MY MAN IN ANTIBES

GETTING TO KNOW GRAHAM GREENE

A Memoir

MICHAEL MEWSHAW

Boston | GODINE | 2023

Published in 2023 by
GODINE
Boston, Massachusetts

LIBRARY OF CONGRESS CONTROL NUMBER: 2022949991
ISBN: 978-1-56792-719-1

First Printing, 2023
Printed in the United States of America

Again for Linda,
and for my second grandson,
Conrad Flynn Mewshaw

In memory of Philip Mayer

MY MAN IN ANTIBES

I

∞

GRAHAM GREENE CHARACTERIZED a writer's childhood as the bank account he draws on for the rest of his creative life. Lucky for him he was born into a family of wealth and prominence. One relative earned a fortune from Brazilian coffee, another operated a lucrative brewing company and owned a Caribbean plantation worked by hundreds of enslaved people. The enslaver's son sired more than a dozen children by Black women, leaving Graham Greene with mixed-race relatives on the island of St. Kitts. What nascent author could ask for richer narrative possibilities?

Raised in genteel comfort an hour outside of London, in Berkhamsted, where his father was the headmaster of a public (i.e., private) school, Greene boasted celebrated authors Robert Lewis Stevenson and Christopher Isherwood on different branches of his family tree. At Oxford, he displayed precocious literary talent, as did his classmates Evelyn Waugh, Harold Acton, L. P. Hartley, and Edward Sackville-West. As a child, he rarely came into contact with the likes of me except when his nurse pushed his pram along the

Berkhamsted Canal and the ragged sons of boatmen shouted obscenities at the little toff.

My father worked for the U.S. postal service and drove a cab on the side. I was raised by a stepfather who managed a laundry and dry-cleaning plant for the U.S. Navy and worked part time as a bartender. Home was on the outskirts of Washington, D.C., in Prince Georges County, Maryland, in a blue-collar suburb then as mercilessly segregated as Mississippi. The surrounding countryside might once have resembled rural England, with forests alternating with rolling pastures, but in the post-WWII real estate boom, bulldozers flattened the trees and scalped the hills to prepare the ground for semi-detached houses. Before sod and twiglike shrubs were planted, the community resembled the Third World villages where Greene set his novels. In wet weather, the bare red clay had the consistency of quicksand; in dry seasons, it acquired a brittle crust, like a laterite road, a scribble in the dust.

I have no memory of life with my father. My mother sent him a Dear John letter while he served in the Army during WWII. His barely literate, bizarrely punctuated response was among the papers my mother willed to me upon her death. The letter made no mention of her primary accusation against him—that he was a profligate gambler who had lost their house in a card game.

After their divorce, I teetered as if on a tight rope between my parents. Each of them poisoned me against the other and badgered me to report the intimacies of their second marriages. I eventually felt I had no choice but to betray them both in order to be true to myself. In this respect, as in others, I pictured similarities between me and Graham Greene, who as a schoolboy was torn between his father, the strict head-master, and his schoolmates, who suspected that he reported their every infraction, especially their sexual vices.

My mother, saddled with two sons under the age of five, hooked up with Tommy Dunn, a sailor who had just mustered out of the military. Too late she learned that he was as reckless a drinker as her first husband had been a gambler. She and Tommy had savage fights, shouting and shoving and punching each other, sometimes drawing blood. But Tommy never hit me or my siblings—unlike Mom, who was an expert at absorbing and at dishing out pain.

When it dawned on me what kind of patrimony I had inherited, I suspected that if an author's childhood was his bank account, I had been shortchanged. To have any chance at becoming a novelist, I would need to switch banks or transfer my meager assets to a different currency. Yet I kept imagining connections between Graham Greene and me, and thought that his writing career might be a template for mine.

Of course this thought came later. As a kid I never heard of Graham Greene. It wasn't until my junior year at St. John DeMatha Catholic High School that an English teacher spoke of *The Power and the Glory* as the quintessential Catholic novel. Rather than assign the book, he had the class watch a televised adaptation of it on Play of the Week. In that era, when serious depictions of religion rarely made it onto primetime TV, *The Power and the Glory* stunned me with its discussion of Catholic dogma embedded in a plot that had the propulsive momentum of a thriller.

A nameless Mexican priest flees persecution by a government dedicated to stamping out the Church. As his survival and his salvation hang in the balance, he hides in remote villages, haunted by his conscience. Far from an exemplary priest, he's an alcoholic who has violated his vow of chastity and had a child. Although there is no priest to forgive him, he retains the power to offer absolution to others, and even in a state of mortal sin he can transform bread and wine into the body and blood of Christ. In the ultimate irony, when the whisky priest is captured and executed, he becomes a martyr, which, according to Catholic doctrine, means he's miraculously assumed into heaven.

The real miracle to me was that Greene managed to make what might otherwise have been an academic debate about faith into a deeply human drama played out in a beleaguered landscape. Its literary merits mattered less than its personal impact. With the kind of fervor available only to an impressionable adolescent, Catholicism seemed a barbed fishhook buried in my flesh. I felt responsible not just for saving my own soul, but also for bringing my divorced parents and my stepfather back to the sacraments. Greene's novel gave me hope that if the whisky priest could be redeemed, so could they.

IN HIS ELUSIVE, elliptical autobiography, *A Sort of Life*, Greene claimed his earliest memory was of a dead dog cooling at the foot of his pram. His sister's pug had been run over and Graham's nurse decided to wheel the mangled corpse home. This image of an animal carcass in a baby carriage, Greene suggested, foreshadowed his troubled life and his career of writing murder mysteries, bleak spy thrillers, and novels set amid the mayhem of the Third World.

A dead dog in a baby carriage struck me as thin gruel compared to the writer's meat in my daily childhood diet. Fifty yards from my front door, the Washington–Baltimore Parkway rounded a dangerous curve, and drivers crashed through the guardrail regular as rent. Hearing the shriek of metal on metal, my mother would herd her four kids up to the accident, as if it were our duty to reckon the number of injured and dead. She regarded these appalling scenes as teachable moments, brutal lessons that speed kills and that drinking and driving—an offense Tommy Dunn committed every day—was the devil's work.

Unlike Greene, who fainted at the sight of blood—he was also terrified of birds and of drowning—I never flinched. Still, these incidents stayed with me, as did the hideous death that occurred in the creek across from our house. Normally a clear trickle, the water became a frothing current during downpours and dug out deep pools. A five-year-old boy stumbled into one of these holes and disappeared. I started in after him, but too soon turned back. I dreaded going in deeper and touching his cold flesh. I cowered on the creek bank until the rescue squad arrived and hauled out the kid's body, stiff and white-bellied as a gigged frog. Secretly I believed I could have/should have saved him. I felt that cowardice kept me from going in over my head.

I never had any such illusions about saving other people in our community, a blighted landscape of hard living and all too often of dying. Married couples took their slugfests out onto the front lawn, as if for the entertainment of neighbors. Infidelity, proved or simply suspected, provoked swift retribution. One husband beat his wife to death with a baseball bat, then killed their baby.

Shit, as the saying goes, happens everywhere, but it piled up higher in that luck-starved place. A little blind girl went door to door singing "I'm Sorry," in imitation of Brenda Lee, and begging for nickels and dimes. Another girl, cruelly disfigured by fire, hid indoors until her skin grafts healed into a lurid brocade of scars. A young boy got hit by a car and afterward hobbled along with his legs locked in metal braces. A boy of about the same age had had a tracheotomy and breathed and squeaked barely intelligible words through a tube in his throat.

By his own vivid account, Graham Greene had barely survived an agonizing childhood. Wracked by alternating currents of anxiety and suicidal depression, he wrote that he had once had a perfectly healthy tooth pulled, counting on anesthesia to provide temporary relief from his emotional turmoil. According to Greene's biographers, this story was probably bogus. The same might have been the case with Greene's celebrated account of playing Russian roulette. His brother, who owned the pistol, pointed out that it had no ammunition. Still, Greene scholars contend that the anecdote, even if false, was a metaphor for his lifelong flirtation with self-destruction.

I had no cause to question the seriousness of Greene's suicidal tendency. As an adolescent I had already seen friends throw their lives away. An eleven-year-old kid, no more, no less nutty than others in the neighborhood, fed his father's .22 rifle barrel into his mouth but succeeded only in blowing off his jaw. Another fellow, a fanatic as we all were about cars, carried his autoeroticism to the extreme of stealing a tractor-trailer and beating off on the upholstery. He ended up in prison, where he killed himself.

Not all of the disturbed acquaintances among my friends turned their anger inward. At the age of fifteen, Wayne Dresbach gunned down his parents and was sentenced to life in prison. His fourteen-year-old brother, Lee, who had witnessed the killings, moved in with my family, adding another combustible element to an already unstable situation.

My mother treated Lee as she did her own children. Depending on her bipolar moods, she smothered him with affection or slapped his face beet red. Consistency was never a virtue she mastered. Still, she never wavered in her commitment to the Dresbach boys. Because no relative stepped forward to help them, she took it on herself to shelter one orphan and rescue the other from life behind bars. When she discovered that Wayne had been physically and sexually abused by his parents, she convinced the court to transfer him from the state penitentiary to Patuxent Institute for Defective Delinquents, where he received psychotherapy and qualified for early release. Unfortunately, it never dawned on her that she and Tommy, along with the rest of us, might have benefited from therapy.

In a sense, we all went to jail with Wayne Dresbach. From the moment of his arrest, my family spent an ungodly amount of time in police stations and holding pens. In the absence of suitable juvenile facilities, Wayne was initially confined to a county jail isolated from the general prison population. My mother argued that this constituted solitary confinement and persuaded the police to let us visit him in his cell, where we sat for hours, mostly in silence, assaulted by the stench of an open toilet and the shouts of other prisoners.

Wayne seemed zoned out, maybe medicated, his eyes dull, his fingertips trembling. Mom gave him a cigarette, something she would never have done with another fifteen-year-old. I couldn't decide what would be worse—Wayne's crushing guilt at killing his parents or the enormous weight on Lee of having watched them die. Later, when I read *Brighton Rock*, Graham

Greene's icy portrait of Pinkie, the teenage assassin hell-bent on losing his soul and dragging his girl down with him, I had no trouble believing that some souls could be saved only through the mystery of God's grace.

As FIRST GRADERS, most children are taught to sing their ABCs. Tommy Dunn taught me how to box. As a preschooler, I was already having fights, and after a kid kneed me in the nuts hard enough to put me in the hospital, Tommy decided I'd better learn to defend myself. He matched me against my older brother, Pat, who hated fighting and ended up hating me for beating him every time Tommy laced the gloves on us. Tommy set up bouts with other boys in the neighborhood, and while I didn't always win, I never backed down, not even after he overmatched me with somebody who broke my nose. At the age of ten, I hit a kid at recess and knocked his front teeth through his lower lip. As punishment, the nun in charge of discipline gave the still bleeding boy a free shot at me.

I never regarded myself as a bully. I never picked fights. I felt I just defended myself. These days, school administrators would recognize that I had "anger management issues" and probably expel me. But at that time and place, fighting was considered a masculine rite of passage. My high school's annual Father and Son Smoker featured boxing matches where boys settled scores for the amusement of the faculty and student body.

I remember a football game when I sat in the bleachers seething as a rival school, a military academy, ran up the score. During halftime, their marching band took the field, beautifully uniformed, parading from end zone to end zone in precise formation, led by a drum major wearing a shako and wielding a baton. This inflamed me. I raced onto the gridiron, intending to barrel into the cadets and wipe the supercilious smiles off their faces.

But the drum major pounced on me. Boney and tall, he seized me by the shoulders and gave me a rough shake. On instinct, I threw a punch, knocking off his shako and exposing his bald freckled skull. A rickety Ichabod Crane character, he collapsed like a skeleton cut down from a noose. All around the stadium, there was an in-suck of breath, an audible expression of horror at what I had done.

For an instant, I was paralyzed. Then I sprinted off the field while the crowd booed and jeered. I didn't slow down until I got to the parking lot, where cars concealed me from everything except my shame.

My mother taunted me: "You're such a tough guy, why don't you protect me from Tommy?" The next time they fought I stepped between them. He tried to push me aside. I pushed back and he stumbled, as much from drunkenness as anything I had done. It was awful to see my boxing instructor cowering on the floor, looking up at the monster he had created. "I changed your diapers," Tommy bleated. "I don't deserve this."

UNLIKE MY ADOLESCENT delinquencies, Graham Greene's schoolboy escapades were international in scope. Shortly after WWI, he volunteered to smuggle currency to the Germans in the French-occupied Rhineland. Then he suggested acting as a double agent for the French. In *A Sort of Life*, he acknowledged that "at that age [eighteen] I was ready to be a mercenary in any cause so long as I was repaid with excitement and a little risk. I suppose too that every novelist has something in common with a spy: he watches, he overhears, he seeks motives and analyzes character, and in his attempt to serve literature he is unscrupulous."

My call to serve literature came when a couple of odd-balls pitched up in the house next to ours. Migrating from New England, they couldn't have seemed weirder if they had crash-landed from Ultima Thule. Neither of them smoked or drank. They didn't own a TV set, and although they had a car, the husband never worked on it, never even washed it. He described himself as a spelunker, and when that furrowed our brows, he explained that he explored caves. Every weekend, he slung a coiled rope over his shoulder, clapped a miner's helmet on his head, and rappelled into caverns.

In his absence, his wife perched at the kitchen table, wearing pedal pushers and a man's untucked shirt, and typed on a rackety Underwood. Stationed at the back door, I looked over through a mesh screen.

"What are you doing?" I asked.

"Writing a book," she said.

"Mind if I watch?" In the fifth grade, I was still reading at a first-grade level. During the summer, I had to take remedial courses. The nuns guessed that a bout of childhood polio had left me with a learning disability. But suddenly I was obsessed with writing as I watched the woman's fingers fly over the keyboard. Words, sentences, whole paragraphs magically appeared on a page that had been empty one instant, then overflowing the next.

Talking and typing at the same time, she said a housewife in New Hampshire, no different from her, had written a novel that transformed her into a millionaire. No, *Peyton Place* wasn't a book for a boy my age, but it proved what you could do once you mastered the craft.

Her mention of "craft" brought to mind braiding lanyards, hand-weaving potholders, gluing Popsicle sticks together into fans. All these things I had already done. What was to keep me from learning to be a writer?

But at the start, I was stymied by the search for a plot. For inspiration, I leafed through a parochial school publication, *My Weekly Reader*, and cannibalized its cartoons, lifting dialogue verbatim from speech bubbles and swiping whole scenes. Yet gradually these stolen elements evolved into a story all my own. It was an eerie experience, unlike anything I had ever done before—except perhaps ripping the wings off June bugs, transforming airborne insects into earthbound scuttlers. For a child raised in a community where whirl was king, where people were blind or disabled or unstable, it was a game-changer to discover I could shape reality to suit myself.

The neighboring housewife never did become a bestselling author. She bolted back to New England when the news broke that her spelunking husband was a bigamist. Instead of exploring caves, he shacked up on weekends with a second wife and family. Spelunking lived on in local slang for deviance.

During grade school and high school and on into college, I tended the flame of my literary aspirations. I churned out poems and short stories, a couple of novellas, and a three-hundred-page manuscript that was less a novel than a turgid travelogue. None of this showed particular talent or won any prizes in college writing contests. At most I received grudging praise for my diligence and gentle remonstrance for the plain-Jane carpentry of my prose. While often disappointed, I could never be dissuaded. Blind faith drove me on.

Graham Greene would have understood. A convert to Catholicism, frequently on the verge of despair, he had chosen to join a tribe that ranked low on the English social ladder. He had done this to persuade a devout woman to marry him. But afterward he found himself a prisoner, not just of his wedding vows, but also of the quirks of canonical law and a wavering belief that became the foundation of his fiction.

Never a conventional believer, Greene tiptoed perpetually along the cliff's edge between heresy and excommunication. Ironically, however, his novels provided moral guidance for millions of traditional Catholics. To his chagrin, even doubting priests sought his counsel, and lost souls regarded him as a general in what Greene called "the church's Foreign Legion."

A conscientious, rule-abiding Catholic myself, I nevertheless admired Greene's struggle with disbelief and respected his intellectual jujitsu in becoming both a writer and a Catholic. That he managed to achieve his literary stature while at the same time coping with constant emotional turmoil struck me as a double triumph.

To top it off, Greene was a man of action as well as ideas, an *engagé* author who empathized with the poor and disenfranchised. Rather than merely pay lip service, he visited the most benighted spots on earth. Some scholars dubbed the bleak settings of his novels *Greeneland*, as if he had fantasized the frightening end-of-the road settings where his characters worked out their fates in fear and trembling. But they were real places, and I vowed to explore them myself, convinced that a certain kind of exotic experience led inevitably to literature.

In a line that resonated for me, Greene wrote, "My roots are in rootlessness." Travel was what a writer was supposed to do—flee the boredom of the mundane, and in my case escape from my family. Because I had little money, I started as a teenager thumbing from coast to coast, crisscrossing the country and hitchhiking into Mexico, imagining myself walking on the wild side.

Not that my schoolboy adventures bore any resemblance to Graham Greene's arduous journeys. He trekked through unmapped jungles in Liberia and Sierra Leone, investigating modern-day slavery; he joined Gurkha troops tracking rebels through the mangroves of Malaysia; he covered the Mau-Mau uprising in Kenya and was pinned down on the Suez Canal during an Israeli–Egyptian exchange of gunfire that killed sixty-two people; he smuggled supplies to Castro's men in Cuba; he traveled repeatedly to Vietnam, first under the French occupation, then under the violent American intervention. He had done all this not simply to gather material for his fiction, but instead to ward off depression and to forget temporarily the chaos of his personal life.

In the summer of my sophomore year of college, I decided to raise the ante of my risk-taking and signed on as a deckhand on a fifty-seven-foot skipjack bound from Solomons Island, Maryland, to St. Thomas in the U.S. Virgin Islands. I had had no previous sailing experience but the owner and captain of the skipjack didn't regard this as a drawback. Apart from a course at a community college in navigation, he had no seagoing knowledge himself. A shakedown cruise on the Chesapeake Bay ended with him crashing his boat into a wharf. This should have scared me into canceling my trip. Instead it convinced me that the captain was in no position to judge my inadequacies.

We both depended on an oysterman who had toiled aboard the skipjack for decades. Not that he had ever sailed beyond the Chesapeake Bay. Although a flat-bottomed skipjack with a shallow-draft centerboard was perfect for dredging oysters, none of us realized how woefully ill-equipped it was for the Atlantic Ocean.

Undaunted by storm warnings, we rounded Cape Hatteras in gale-force winds that shredded the sails and left us at the mercy of an auxiliary engine that barely had the muscle to head us into the monstrous waves. I was too seasick to be scared. Bent over the taffrail, I tossed my cookies and kept on gagging after I had nothing more to give.

We worked in shifts, four hours on, four hours off. I never slept below deck. In this I followed the example of the oysterman, who alone had the good sense to admit he was terrified. Wrapping up in a tarpaulin, he kept a bleary-eyed vigil night and day.

The captain stayed serenely calm even after the ship-to-shore radio shorted out and the compass shut down. Steering by dead reckoning, he headed west, figuring we'd eventually hit the coast. After three days, we put in at Georgetown, South Carolina, and Coast Guard officials greeted us at the dock. It wasn't a welcoming committee. They impounded the skipjack and refused to permit it out of the harbor until it complied with basic safety regulations.

The oysterman jumped ship, which gave me the gumption to do the same. It came to me what Graham Greene must have learned early on—while some journeys provide the raw material for novels, others just leave you sick to your stomach.

Like Greene, D. H. Lawrence was a hectic traveler, ever on the search for a climate that would heal his tubercular lungs and a landscape that would nourish his soul. He subscribed to the belief that the most perilous and potentially transformative journey was a man's exploration of a woman's body. Greene would surely have agreed. Although he remained married to his wife, Vivien, his whole life, Greene had an unappeasable appetite for women. In a candid letter to Vivien as they were separating, he confessed that "by my nature, my selfishness, even to some degree by my profession, I should always and with anyone, have been a bad husband."

An early draft of *A Sort of Life* contained a list of forty-seven of his favorite prostitutes. This list was deleted from the final draft, and there's not much in the published manuscript about his affairs with Dorothy Glover and Catherine Walston, a married mother of six children who asked Greene to be her godfather when she converted to Catholicism. Though Greene called Walston the love of his life, he cheated on her just as he did on his other mistresses. It's commonly assumed that Walston was the model for Sarah in *The End of the Affair*. No doubt she appreciated that literary tribute far more than she did Greene's naming a Haitian brothel in *The Comedians* "Mère Catherine's."

Hypersexuality was one aspect of Greene's life that I had no desire to emulate. Born into the smoldering ashes of my mother's first marriage, coming of age in the scalding flames of her second, I yearned for a loving, faithful partner. At the age of twenty-one, I thought I had found her in a coed at the University of Maryland. Unlike her sorority sisters, she was smart, well read, and interested in writing. Three months after we met, long before we were sexually intimate, we started discussing marriage.

Then her interest in me seemed to wobble. When I asked why, she revealed that she was pregnant by another guy. She swore she didn't love him, she loved me. Although abortion was illegal in 1964, she presumed that somebody from my slummy background must know how to arrange one. I didn't.

Plan B—standard procedure in those days—was for an unmarried pregnant girl to give birth and put her baby up for adoption. My girlfriend declared that she couldn't do this in the Washington, D.C., area, where her parents were socially prominent and had lofty expectations for her future. Without much thought, we cobbled together a plan to move to California, where I'd support her until the baby was born.

As a graduation present, her parents gave her a new Thunderbird, which she drove to San Francisco. There, she volunteered for the Republican National Convention. To save money for our life together, I worked that summer, first as a truck driver for Pepsi Cola, then as a hash-slinging trainee at Hot Shoppe. In September, we rendezvoused in Los Angeles, where I landed a job as a desktop calculator salesman. I wore a suit and tie every day, and gave a pitch-perfect imitation of the kind of adult I had every dread of becoming.

In January 1965, after the baby was delivered and adopted and we had started the return trip to the East Coast, I suggested we detour into Mexico. The girl was game—as long as we garaged her T-Bird on the U.S. side of the border.

An overnight bus delivered us to Durango, where we hitched a ride heading west for the Pacific. Beneath a mountain range lush with palm trees, banana plants, and colorful scrolls of bougainvillea huddled poverty-stricken villages that might have been lifted intact from the pages of *The Power and the Glory*. Deep in Greeneland, I fumbled to explain to my girlfriend that this was how I wanted to spend my life—not as the surrogate hubby who had hawked desktop calculators in

California, but instead traveling to obscure places and storing up impressions for my fiction.

Not for the first time, nor the last, I misread my audience. The girl soon got her fill of the Third World and apparently of me. A one-eyed pilot flew us in a crop duster back to the States, where we retrieved the T-Bird and set out across the sere winter plains of Texas. After hours of solemn palaver, she dropped me off at Love Field in Dallas, and I flew alone to Maryland.

ALONG WITH LOSING the girl, I almost lost my grip. Clinging on by my fingernails, I completed my undergraduate degree and dithered over the future. A stint in Vietnam, I mused, might be what a young novelist needed. Southeast Asia had supplied Graham Greene with a surfeit of material. Of course he had traveled there as a journalist with a return ticket, not as a grunt who might be transported back in a body bag. And he hadn't had to kill anybody. Somehow that struck me as worse than losing my own life—extinguishing someone else's.

Grad school was the conventional haven for guys my age who lacked the guts to flee to Canada. High scores on the Graduate Record Exam won me a grant I had never heard of, a National Defense Act Fellowship. In effect, the U.S. Department of Defense paid me to dodge the draft, and the University of Virginia English Department supplied a matching grant.

For someone of sounder mind, this might have prompted a celebration. For me, it provoked an insuperable urge to escape. I bought a discounted student ticket, caught a plane to Puerto Rico, and with fifty bucks in my billfold hopped an interisland ferry to West End, Tortola, in the British Virgins. Back then the town consisted of a raw concrete landing next to a clutch of cinder-block hovels. There was no electricity, no telephone, no paved roads, no drinking water except for rain collected in rooftop cisterns. Privies filled the air with the prevailing odor of pee.

I fell in with a couple of drunken fishermen who had been hired by an American heiress to the Dodge family fortune to babysit her six-year-old autistic son. She had parked the boy outside the States to prevent his father, one of her half a dozen ex-husbands, from petitioning the court for custody and cutting himself in for a share of her money.

Allowed to freeload as long as I liked, I slept on the living room couch and dulled my guilt with local rum that cost a dollar a bottle. Then a different rich American woman arrived and ruined the fragile equilibrium of the summer. In an alcohol-fueled frenzy, one of the fishermen beat her to a bloody pulp. This was a scene I had witnessed at home all too often. I pried him off for fear he'd kill her. Then fearing he'd kill me, I ended my idyll in the Caribbean.

I SHOWED UP in Charlottesville that September an emotional wreck, registered for classes, and promptly decided to drop out. Before I left, I felt the need to speak to a priest, the only counsel available without an appointment or proof of insurance. At the UVA Newman Center, Father Hickey, dressed in street clothes, sat with me on the front steps and listened as I spilled a garbled account of the pregnant girlfriend, the stint in L.A., the breakup in Mexico, followed by months of mooching off an innocent child. Drilling down into the past, I described my abusive bipolar mother, my alcoholic stepfather, and my detached biological father who commented on my Phi Beta Kappa key, "That and a dime will buy you a cup of coffee."

Who knows how long I might have nattered on if Father Hickey hadn't interrupted. "Son," he told me, "you're really very sick. Let me put you in touch with a psychiatrist at Student Health."

If he feared his bluntness would hurt me, he was badly mistaken. Profuse in my gratitude, I babbled what a relief it was to learn I was crazy. I had imagined that the world, which I had no chance of changing, was mad. But with help, I hoped I could change myself.

II

<small>◇◇◇◇◇◇</small>

LINDA KIRBY AND I met on a blind date on January 22, 1966, a landmark day not simply for that meeting, but also because a blizzard buried the grounds of UVA. This rare meteorological phenomenon was the capstone to a string of improbable episodes.

Linda's phone number had come to me via a Spanish professor at a women's college shortly before he made a drunken, fumbling pass at me. After our first conversation, she and I corresponded for months. To a letter she sent me in French, I replied with an unattributed quote from *The Magic Mountain*, a long passage where Thomas Mann switches from German to French to describe a woman's beautiful tubercular body. This convinced Linda to visit me in Charlottesville.

Chronically broke, I had to borrow money from fellows in the graduate student dorm. I also had to borrow clothing. My habitual wardrobe consisted of cast-offs that my stepfather filched from the Lost and Found Department of the Naval Receiving Station laundry. His accounts included Walter Reed Hospital, which was crammed with Marines recovering from traumatic wounds they had suffered in Vietnam. Some didn't survive, and their families failed to collect their freshly cleaned clothes. Long accustomed to hand-me-downs—my mother forced me as a kid to wear my deceased grandmother's green-and-white saddle oxfords to Easter Mass—I had nothing against dead people's clothes.

But meeting Linda Kirby was a special occasion, and I needed wardrobe assistance. She endeared herself to me by not noticing—or politely not mentioning—that my trousers and sport coat didn't match. When it emerged at dinner that I was revising a manuscript I had scrawled by hand, Linda volunteered that she typed eighty words a minute and would be glad to help out. I should mention that she was tall and slim and lovely and whip-smart. After that evening, we never dated anyone else.

When eventually I informed her I was in therapy, Linda seemed fascinated rather than fearful or disapproving. She listened as attentively as the psychiatrist to stories of my childhood. With the same equanimity, she accepted that I had no money and probably never would. I intended to become a novelist, and I told her if I were lucky, I'd probably end up teaching creative writing. But at least college professors enjoyed long vacations, which would leave me free to travel and write.

Linda assured me she loved to travel. She had spent her junior year in Paris and had roamed around Europe, including a month behind the Iron Curtain, where in those Cold War days few Americans ventured. She was fluent in French, Spanish, and Italian and promised to serve as my tour guide.

I cautioned Linda that my idea of travel might differ from hers. The term *travel*, I pedantically explained, had the same linguistic roots as *travail*, and for ages it had been synonymous with a quasi-religious quest for enlightenment. I loaned her my dog-eared copy of *The Power and the Glory* and urged her to read it and join me in Mexico that summer. Secretly I viewed the trip as an exorcism and a test—an exorcism of the girl-friend for whom Mexico was a deal-breaker and a test of Linda's commitment to an impecunious author.

For three hundred bucks I bought a 1959 Saab, a Swedish automobile with a two-cycle engine as underpowered as a lawn mower. Each full tank of fuel had to be topped up with of a quart of oil. South of the border, Mexican mechanics objected that we'd be incinerated, but Linda reassured them in flawless Spanish that there was no danger.

Actually, there was plenty of danger. We slept beside the road and ate in cheap cantinas, risking alimentary distress. Further tempting fate and straining the Saab's stamina, we puttered across the Sierra Madre Occidental and descended through breath-catching *barrancas* to Acapulco. Even then it was an overpriced, overdeveloped resort. So we pushed on to Pie de la Cuesta and a bamboo beach hut that trembled after each towering wave pounded the shore. No exaggeration, the earth moved for us.

As if following an alphabetical algorithm, we plotted a course from Acapulco to Zihuatanejo on an unpaved road that forded rivers and crunched through fields strewn with drying copra. Free of tourists except for a few proto-hippies high on the premium local weed and holdovers from Timothy Leary's LSD experiments in the early 1960s, Zihuatanejo had a single hotel with a caged jaguar in the lobby. Linda loved everything—Mexican food and beer, tequila taken neat with a lick of salt from the back of her hand, fresh-baked bread and wild honey at breakfast. She didn't even mind the jaguar's miasmal smell. Then I challenged her to come skin diving.

A fisherman on the Playa de Ropa owned odds and ends of snorkeling equipment and agreed to run us out to an island a mile offshore. In the placid water of the bay, the boat spanked along at a fast clip. Perched on the bow, flawless as a figurehead, Linda gestured to a palm-fringed speck of sand at the horizon. To me it looked a lot farther than a mile away, and beyond the sheltered bay, to my immense embarrassment, I realized I was going to be seasick, a déjà vu of the dreadful trip around Cape Hatteras. As I retched over the side, the fisherman laughed, and Linda scolded him in Spanish.

I waved off her suggestion that we skip the skin diving, and once we reached dry land, I demonstrated how to scrub the lens of her mask with spit to prevent it from fogging up. Then I told her to wet the inside of her flippers so they would slide easily onto her feet. I warned that if we spotted a shark, she shouldn't panic, she should stay behind me. Finally, cradling the speargun to my chest, I marched us into the water.

Immediately a fat, slow-moving fish floated in front of me. I mistook it for a grouper and zinged it with the spear just behind its gills. It shape-changed into a cannonball, a dead weight bristling with spines. It was a blowfish that tugged me toward the bottom, flailing at the end of the spear, thrashing to break free. I managed to wrestle it onto the beach, where the fisherman beat it to death with a marlin spike, hollering the whole time that I owed him extra for ruining his spear.

On the turbulent return to Zihuatanejo, I sagged over the side again and sicked up bile. Linda took charge. She was the Hemingway type, I realized, gifted with grace under fire and competence on all occasions, whereas I was a tender bud in the Lady Brett Ashley mode. Dear reader, she married me.

UNDER THE SWAY of *The Comedians*, Linda and I decided to honeymoon in Haiti, the Nightmare Republic, as Greene called it, a country ruled by the murderous President-for-life Papa Doc Duvalier. We registered at the Hotel Oloffson, the disintegrating gingerbread palace where Greene had set his novel. There we met Aubelin Jolicoeur, the diminutive, self-styled society columnist whom Greene portrayed as Petit Pierre, a slightly silly, slightly sinister spy who monitored foreign guests.

Deep in the hills behind Port-au-Prince, a voodoo ceremony was presented to us, the only white people there, as authentic black magic. Who knows? The next day, in a Quonset hut whose tin roof rang out with rain, we attended Sunday Mass, which dragged on almost as long as the voodoo ceremony, its singing as hypnotic as the chanting in the mountains.

On our last night, the electricity blinked off and the staff locked the Oloffson's gates and ordered guests to stay indoors. Rumors spread that there had been a coup. The next day we learned it was a false alarm. During a domestic squabble chez Duvalier, the dictator's wife had locked Papa Doc in the bathroom, and he pressed a button that flooded Port-au-Prince with his henchmen, the Tonton Macoutes.

IF FOLLOWING IN Graham Greene's footsteps sounds foolish, I'll plead in self-defense that I had plenty of company. For decades, readers and religious zealots, defrocked priests, respected scholars, and admiring fellow authors had formed a procession behind Greene, like penitents on the Via Dolorosa. Norman Sherry, Greene's chosen biographer, traced his subject's convoluted route around the world. The result was a prodigious, three-volume study and a cruel litany of medical traumas. In the course of Sherry's nomadic research, he contracted dysentery and malaria and was obliged to have a gangrenous section of his intestines surgically removed. Although the project almost killed him, Sherry wrote: "I was the nearest thing to being a son to [Greene] . . . I often felt I must be him." This prompted a competing biographer to speculate that Sherry suffered from dementia.

No one ever accused Gloria Emerson of being soft in the head. A National Book Award–winning journalist who had covered the Vietnam War for the *New York Times*, she had a reputation for hard-nosed professionalism and stiletto-like precision. Yet she revealed a treacly streak for Graham Greene. After producing an adulatory profile of him for *Rolling Stone*, she wrote a novel, *Loving Graham Greene*, about a woman who rushes to Algeria during an Islamic insurrection to support indigenous authors.

Pico Iyer, a highly regarded English novelist and essayist who lives as an expatriate in Japan, would appear to have little in common with Greene except an addiction to travel. A spiritual rather than a conventionally religious man, Iyer is a devotee of the Dalai Lama and projects in person an aura of Zen-like gentleness, not at all like Greene's feistiness. Yet in *The Man Within My Head*, a play on the title of Greene's first novel, he portrays Greene, whom Iyer never met, as an uncanny mirror of his own past and a figure of prophecy for his future.

Among Greene's fans, there are an astounding number who claimed to *be* him. In the epilogue to *Ways of Escape*, Greene attempted to tease out the mystery of these doppel-

gängers. Some angled for money; others harbored a mythoma-
niacal craving for celebrity. They showed up uninvited at literary festivals; they granted interviews to unsuspecting reporters;
they dispatched letters to the editor under his signature. They
rang his telephone number and declared themselves to be the
genuine Graham Greene and him an imposter.

One lawbreaker in India made headlines: "Graham
Greene convicted. Sentenced to two years' rigorous imprisonment." An African author didn't bother stealing Greene's
identity. He stole an entire Greene novel, *It's a Battlefield*, and
published it in France, where his plagiarism went undetected
until the book won a literary prize. Out of sympathy, Greene
refused to have him prosecuted.

Although I've said I wanted to be Graham Greene, I
should correct that. I wanted to be a writer like Graham
Greene. By temperament and sensibility, not to mention innate
talent, I never dreamed of becoming Joyce or Faulkner. But I
regarded Graham Greene as a reasonable goal, until years of
failure taught me the truth. Greene's deceptively simple style
and straightforward storytelling are as hard-worked and finely
wrought as hammered silver.

IN THE FIRST year of our marriage, Linda and I lived in a
converted chicken coop fifteen miles outside of Charlottesville. Once again I might be accused of aping Graham Greene,
who early on with Vivien leased a thatch-roofed cottage in the
Cotswolds that was infested by rats. Squirrels scurried in the
walls of our chicken coop. Not as bad as rats, but close.

The plan was for me to postpone my doctoral dissertation
and finish a novel about—no surprise!—a road trip to Mexico.

Depending on my NDEA grant for daily expenses, we banked Linda's salary from teaching junior high school French and saved for what she hoped would be a return to Paris. She encouraged me to apply for a Fulbright. Although my novel in progress would never qualify for a sabbatical in France, she was confident I could concoct a grant-winning project.

I submitted the synopsis for a novel about the relationship between Paul Verlaine and Arthur Rimbaud, a couple of roguish nineteenth-century poets who scandalized French literary society by running away together. Rimbaud had been barely seventeen years old, Verlaine an established author with a wife and child. The *coup de foudre* concluded with Verlaine shooting Rimbaud in the arm and ending up in jail. After his release, Rimbaud disappeared into Africa, never to write poetry again. Having caught verse like a virus, he passed the disease on to others, but was cured of it forever himself.

Another hurdle confronted me, not a negligible one. I didn't speak French. While I had studied it for two years in high school and three in college, it had been taught at both levels as if it were a dead language, like Latin. By dint of memorization, I mastered the grammar and conjugations and crammed for vocabulary tests with the aid of flash cards. Still, I couldn't have conducted a conversation with a kindergartner.

Linda assured me we could deal with that difficulty once the Fulbright Commission made its decision. But when we learned that my application had been approved, we were too busy celebrating to worry about anything as paltry as my ignorance of French. After we calmed down, a more pressing dilemma presented itself. How could we afford to spend a year in Paris?

The Fulbright stipend totaled twenty-seven hundred dollars and covered my transatlantic transportation in an economy cabin on the SS *France*. We had to pay for Linda's passage out of our own pocket. The fellowship made no provision for married couples beyond supplying a list of *pensiones* in the Latin Quarter that offered cheap room and board. According to my calculations, even if we cut our expenses to the bone, we'd need another five thousand dollars.

Providentially—at least it seemed so at the time—our paths crossed with a Frenchwoman who owned a studio apartment in Paris, convenient to the Sorbonne. She offered to rent it to us in what she referred to as an *"entre amis"* arrangement. This "among friends" deal meant we had no legal contract and paid nine months in advance.

"It's a modest *pied-à-terre*," she said, *"mais très folklorique."* An early chapter of Hemingway's *The Sun Also Rises* was set on her street, and if you leaned out the front window far enough, you could catch a glimpse of Notre-Dame.

Over the summer, while Linda packed our belongings into duffel bags, I sat successfully for my PhD oral exams and submitted my novel, *Man in Motion*, to Albert Erskine, a senior editor at Random House. He replied with a tantalizing letter: "Needless to say, I think you're very good." If I would be patient, he'd get back to me with a definitive answer. Meanwhile, he wondered whether I realized that *Man in Motion* was the title of a critical study of William Faulkner. In a throwaway line, Erskine mentioned that he had been Faulkner's editor.

ACCORDING TO THE Chinese proverb, the longest journey begins with a single step. Ours started with a bus ride to Washington, D.C., on a malodorous Greyhound. There we transferred to Trailways for the trip to the Port Authority, New

York City. Those eight bum-numbing hours on a plastic seat permitted me ample time to spin my wheels. Although I didn't admit it, I was afraid. Afraid that Albert Erskine—Faulkner's former editor, for Christ's sake!—would reject my novel. Afraid I'd be laid low by seasickness on the five-day Atlantic crossing. Afraid that my lousy French would betray me as a fraud. Afraid that with complete freedom to focus on my work, I'd suffer writer's block. Afraid that culture shock would send me cringing back to the United States like a whipped cur.

Against all odds, I didn't vomit a single time on the SS *France*. That heartened me. But we reached Paris to discover that our apartment was on the top floor of a six-story building, *sans ascenseur.* Shouldering one duffel bag after another, I humped up a hundred-step spiral staircase through distinct olfactory zones—garlic, frying fish, Camembert, Asian spices—to what resembled a storage bin rather than a studio.

Our landlady, it appeared, was a pathological hoarder. Before I set down our bags, Linda had to clear space amid mounds of cardboard boxes brimming with childhood memorabilia, bank statements, restaurant menus, opera playbills, souvenir matchbooks, and swizzle sticks. To make room for our clothes, we emptied an armoire of the landlady's duds and a dozen pairs of her down-at-the-heels shoes.

That night in bed, between fever dreams, I wondered how to convince the landlady to refund our money. Abject begging wasn't beneath me. But where would we go if she did release us from our agreement?

The next day, while Linda continued to unpack, I spiraled down the staircase through its pungent smells, planning to come to grips with Paris. But everywhere I went it eluded my grasp. The city demanded constant accommodation. More than that, absolute capitulation. You did things the French way or not at all. Customers were forbidden to touch the fruit and vegetables at street markets. The otherwise lovely parks were patrolled like maximum security prisons. Walking on the grass was strictly *défendu* and the wire-harped chairs were guarded by whiskery old crones who charged twenty centimes to sit down. Most baffling of all, women ruled the men's room.

In theory, I was assigned to the Sorbonne, but the university had no interest in a Fulbright Fellow in creative writing. Still tense after the convulsions of May '68, academic bureaucrats decided I could do whatever I liked. Mostly what I liked was to steer clear of the gendarmes in riot gear who patrolled the grueling *grands boulevards*. Blundering into a student demonstration, I got lashed by rubber truncheons.

In a reversal of the plot of many a classic French novel, I began to view myself as a naive country boy, eager to abandon the city and seek his fortune in the provinces. Since the Sorbonne said I was free to settle anywhere, why, I asked Linda, didn't we move to the Riviera, like Gerald and Sara Murphy and their illustrious guests at the Villa America?

But before we went anywhere, I needed to open a bank account so my minuscule monthly Fulbright stipend could be deposited. Linda considered this a fine opportunity for me to practice French. "If you get stumped, talk around the subject," she said. "Try different vocabulary, different tenses. I'll wait outside."

I chose a *guichet* attended by a woman who looked far too cute to treat a customer cruelly. *"Monsieur?"* she said.

"Bonjour," I said, then blurted out a sentence I had honed for hours. *"Je voudrais ouvrir un con."*

Birdlike, she cocked her head. *"Comment?"*

Enunciating each syllable, I repeated myself.

The girl smiled. *"Encore, s'il vous plaît."*

Abiding by Linda's advice, I reformulated the sentence as a question. *"Est-ce que c'est possible d'ouvrir un con?"*

She laughed into her fist instead of laughing in my face. People in line behind me laughed too. Linda came in to check on me and joined the chuckling chorus.

"We can't all be perfectly fluent," I snapped.

"Oh, but you were fluent," she said. "It's just that you asked to open a cunt."

Thereafter I left the all the banking and the French speaking to Linda.

DAYS AFTER THIS fiasco, rushing to catch the Metro at la place Maubert, I thrust out my left hand to keep the doors from closing. The window glass shattered like a shower of confetti. For a few heartbeats, I felt nothing. My nervous system needed a moment to process the insult I had inflicted upon it. At first, there was no blood, just a crescent-shaped gash on my wrist, the signature of a suicide. Then great pain caught up with me and torrents of blood gushed out. The crowd on the quay groaned in unison.

Pinching the flaps of skin shut, I stumbled upstairs to a pharmacy, where a kind man in a surgeon's smock swaddled me in so much gauze I looked like I was wearing a boxing glove. *"C'est pas grave,"* he soothed me, but added that I'd better get to a hospital. I hailed a taxi and asked to be hurried to the American Hospital, unaware that it lay on the opposite side of the city, in Neuilly.

When blood started seeping through the bandage, the cabbie hollered that I was staining his upholstery. He insisted I hold my hand out the window. At la place des Invalides, we crossed a bridge to the Right Bank and wrought-iron fences flashed by like gold-tipped spears. If I didn't survive, I thought this would be my last bewildering image of Paris.

At the American Hospital, the ER staff were singularly unimpressed by my injury. A nurse told me to remove the bandage and wash my hand at a sink. To keep from fainting, I knelt. The cut on my wrist looked like a puckered mouth blowing bubbles of blood.

A doctor sauntered in, glanced cursorily at the wound, and complimented my cleaning job. As he stitched me up, he counted the number of sutures out loud. When he reached twenty-six, he knotted the thread, then shot an ampoule of anti-tetanus serum into my shoulder. He warned me I might suffer a little soreness. "But you'll have an interesting scar. *Un souvenir de votre visite à Paris.*"

On the cab ride back to the Left Bank, I felt clammy with fever. Too late I learned I was allergic to French tetanus serum. I barely had the strength to climb the stairs and tell Linda to start packing.

III

ONCE WE CLEARED out most of the clutter, we had no trouble subletting the studio to a Fulbright couple, who reimbursed the money we had paid in advance. With this windfall, Linda and I bought a VW and beetled south. We had no plan, no destination. As so often in our itinerant lives, our hearts were helium-filled balloons that dragged us willy-nilly along for the ride.

In somnolent villages, a leaden sky drooped over pollarded trees that lined the roads. Their limbs had been so brutally pruned, they resembled amputated arms that reminded me of my throbbing wrist. Every time I changed the bandages, splinters of glass spiked out of the stitches. I hadn't done such a great job of cleaning the cut after all.

In Cannes, bright flowers flourished under palm trees, suggesting Florida. But the daytime temperature hovered in the 50s, then plunged below freezing at night. Despite the evidence of my senses, I refused to accept the reality of winter on the Riviera. Real estate agents swore that once this freak arctic spell blew over, the beaches would be carpeted with sunbathers. So Linda and I rashly decided to settle on the Côte d'Azur.

There were plenty of seaside rentals available in the off-season. But every place exceeded our budget. We retreated inland, to the *arrière-pays*—the backcountry—where Grasse, Mougins, Vence, and Saint-Paul de Vence were swagged like a jeweled necklace over the hills. Any of these towns would have been perfect for us—if we had had the money.

Auribeau-sur-Siagne, the last and least fashionable *village perché*, boasted no celebrated chefs, no three-star restaurants, no renowned artists or writers. It would have looked utterly abandoned if its stone chimneys hadn't leaked pencil-thin stripes of smoke.

Across the valley from Auribeau, a large Provençal house, *un mas*, as it was called, lorded it over a cluster of cottages. One of these had a small outbuilding that could, a real estate agent advised me, serve as my office. This and the main cottage, he said, had been designed by an architect affiliated with Le Corbusier. The name meant nothing to me. It fell to Linda to confirm that, yes, the two structures bore Corbu's hallmarks—molded concrete walls, slotlike windows and skylights, and an intriguing ensemble of rooms into "a machine for living."

One basic amenity was missing, however. There was no central heating. The real estate agent promised that the fireplace would be adequate to deal with the occasional cold morning. So Linda and I coughed up six months' rent in advance and moved in.

Once it quit raining, the temperature fell and a hard freeze printed ferns of frost on the skylight and turned the tile floors into an ice-skating rink. Linda and I closed off one room after another, draping blankets over the windows. We huddled near the fireplace, wearing knit caps and gloves. Then a snowfall transformed Le Corbusier's "machine for living" into a crypt for dying and rendered my office in the outbuilding unusable.

I spent my days foraging for windfallen wood, chopping it into manageable logs and feeding them to the fireplace. I scavenged dead vines from vineyards and stole sheets of cork oak that had been stacked beside the road. Above all, I treasured olive tree branches, which were fiendishly difficult to light, but once they caught burned for hours.

As the whitewashed face of the fireplace turned as scorched as a frying pan, I imagined the manuscript of *Man in Motion* floating like ashes through the halls of Random House. Even if I had had the gumption to ring Albert Erskine for an update, I couldn't have afforded an international call. In that pre-fax, pre-internet era, I had no choice but to wait.

I marvel that I survived—not just the cold, but also the corrosive doubt. How much of my persistence was sheer egotism? How much self-delusion? Where did it come from, this conviction that I had something to say that deserved to be published? Surely all such nonsense should have been knocked out of my head by now. Instead, I recalled a line by W. H. Auden describing Arthur Rimbaud's childhood in a forbidding French hamlet: "The cold had made a poet." I hoped it might make me a novelist.

Because the VW was our sole reliable source of warmth, we retreated to it on freezing days and ratcheted the heater up full blast. Then we drove randomly around the posh peninsulas of Cap d'Antibes and Saint-Jean-Cap-Ferrat.

We had just one bookish encounter that winter, an evening arranged by the physician who removed my stitches and claimed to be on intimate terms with America's most famous author. He introduced us to Harold Robbins, then at the apogee of his soft porn career. Linda and I had dinner at his villa, where Robbins proudly showed us the office where he narrated his novels into a Dictaphone. He also pointed to his yacht, the longest and most luxurious vessel in the Cannes harbor. But he said he didn't often use it and never went swimming: "I have punctured eardrums."

"I'm sorry," Linda said.

"Don't be. I had them punctured on purpose so I can breathe through them when I'm eating a chick."

Ah, the literary life!

IN PAROCHIAL SCHOOL the nuns used to preach that God never tried a man with afflictions without offering sufficient grace to pass the test. In our case, a *deus ex machina* appeared in the person of Philip Moulton Mayer, who occupied the imposing *mas* up the hill from our igloo. He and his wife, Claire, invited us over for drinks.

A slim man of fifty, Philip sported a crew cut flecked with almost as much gray as I had at the age of twenty-five. By his plummy accent, I pegged him as British or upper-crust Anglo-Irish. But he said he had an American passport, having been born in the States while his parents temporarily resided there. His father was a German Jew who had emigrated to England as a penniless youth and made a fortune in nonferrous metals. Ultimately, Robert Mayer was knighted for financing classical concerts for children.

Philip greeted us that first night at the gates of Montclair, a massive cube of terra cotta–colored stucco, three stories tall, with forest green shutters. As we walked around to the front entrance, I noticed a swimming pool and a tennis court. When Linda asked the size of the property, Philip mumbled a figure in hectares that amounted to seven acres. He seemed almost embarrassed by this abundance and added, as if we had the right to know, that he had bought Montclair with money from his father.

My trailer park pride wouldn't permit me to show I was impressed. Because Sir Robert Mayer was a world-renowned philanthropist, I didn't want Philip to lump us in with the charity cases. As casually as I could, I dropped into the conversation that I was in France on a Fulbright, thinking this would persuade him that we were solvent.

Philip mentioned that he had gone to Harvard; 1968 was the twenty-fifth anniversary of his graduation. Norman Mailer had been a classmate. He hastily admitted that they hadn't been friends. Unlike Mailer, who had famously spent WWII as an infantryman in the Pacific, Philip had had a medical deferment and drove an ambulance in the North African and European theaters.

The interior of Montclair was simple, sparsely furnished and unadorned except for a couple of incongruous artworks that looked like souvenirs from Asia. While Philip poured us a double-malt Scotch, Claire passed around dishes of crackers and pâté, cheese and nuts. What a luxury it was to nibble salted almonds and drink fine whiskey in a room that didn't threaten to cause chilblains!

Philip had little talent—maybe just no tolerance—for small talk. In social situations, he saw no reason not to discuss religion and politics. He made it clear that he didn't support Richard Nixon, who had several weeks earlier been elected U.S. president, and although he wasn't hawkish on Vietnam, he was staunchly anti-communist. As a freelance journalist, he had flown at his own expense to Southeast Asia to report from Saigon and Phnom Penh. Then, during this past spring's Russian invasion of Czechoslovakia, he had driven to Prague to file articles for the *Irish Times*. On the return trip, he had filled his car with a family of Czech refugees whom he put up for months at Montclair.

"Oh, Philip, let's not talk about that," Claire said. She was a tall, stylish woman, still tan from the summer, and spoke English with a French accent: "I'm dying to learn why you two came here and rented a summer cottage in winter."

"The agent swore the fireplace would be sufficient," Linda said.

"The big liar," Claire exclaimed. "Is it true," she asked me, "that you threatened to break his jaw?"

I confessed that I had lost my temper when the water in our toilet froze. "But I never touched the man," I said.

"That's because he jumped out of the window," Linda broke in.

Philip and Claire hooted with laughter.

"His office was on the ground floor," I argued. "He didn't have to jump. He just stepped through an open window and ran."

The Mayers found this unspeakably funny.

"What about the barber in Pégomas?" Philip asked. "What went wrong there?"

"I never said a word to him."

"That's what I heard," Philip said. "The barber claims a beautiful American woman showed up with a deaf man who sat in the chair like a mummy while the woman gave instructions on how to cut his hair. Villagers think you're a brain-damaged Vietnam veteran."

"*Mutilé de guerre*," Claire chimed in.

Under the influence of the excellent Scotch and heartened by the Mayers' company, I accepted my role as butt of the joke and recounted all our tribulations in France. I gave an especially lively description of the incident in the Paris bank.

"But you do intend to learn French, don't you?" Philip asked.

"No, never," I declared theatrically. "As a writer, I don't want to blunt the instrument with which I work."

I had frequently played court jester with my melancholic mother, thinking it was my responsibility to cheer her up. But why was I doing it now? The Mayers must have interpreted it as a *cri de coeur* and they offered help. They owned a portable oil-burning heater—*un poêle à mazout*—which they urged us to install in our fireplace, with a flue up the chimney to carry off the fumes.

At the end of the evening, Philip escorted us to the gate. Passing the tennis court, he asked, "Either of you play?"

We said we didn't.

"You should learn. I could teach you. Let me know whenever you'd like to have a hit."

The cold air was scented with pine, cypress, and eucalyptus. "Sorry you've had such a tough time, but I hope you'll finally like it here," he said. "You know, to visit in summer and claim you love the South of France is like looking at a woman in her fanciest clothes. You might imagine you love her, but you'll never know until you see what's underneath. Winter's when this countryside is stripped bare. If you learn to love it now, you'll be hooked forever."

Normally I resisted such fortune-cookie wisdom, just as I had rejected tennis. Basketball was my game, a scrappy physical contest played in an atmosphere of honest sweat, not starchy white shirts and shorts and country club cologne. With its aura of monkish silence and gentlemanly decorum, tennis felt all wrong for a prole like me. Still, Linda and I decided to give it a try. We bought ten-dollar wooden rackets with plastic strings and leatherette hand grips, and wearing T-shirts and cut-off jeans, we batted balls back and forth while Philip prowled the sidelines, shouting, "Racket back. Bend your knees. Follow through."

Lodged jewel-like in the foothills of the Maritime Alps, the court was perfect for a pair of beginners. The gritty hard surface guaranteed a high bounce and slowed down the ball, making every shot playable if you were ready to run. I came to appreciate why so many writers were devoted to the game. It was a cadenced dance of indirection, part poetry, part well-worked prose.

Linda and I soon advanced from pitty-patting the ball to mixed doubles with Philip and Claire. A relentless retriever, I delighted in keeping the points alive, and some days Linda and I outlasted the Mayers and won a game.

In singles against Philip, I could keep the score close; I suspect he threw points to buck up my spirits. But in the end, he always won. Still, he insisted that he enjoyed our matches and to prove he wasn't just blowing smoke, he proposed a deal. If I promised to practice until I could give him honest competition, he'd let Linda and me use the court whenever we liked. More than that, he'd let us live at Montclair during the months he was away at his house in Ireland.

Even in the late 1960s, villas in the south of France with five bedrooms and five baths and a tennis court and pool rented for a king's ransom. But rather than exult like a lottery winner, I hesitated. This sounded like a con, a bait-and-switch tease. No one gave you something for nothing.

Philip insisted it was a straight give-and-get agreement. He wanted a tennis partner. If I could serve that role, plus offer intelligent conversation, well, he preferred that to paying some bored pro for lessons.

It didn't escape me that Philip regarded me as a protégé. Perhaps "project" is a better term—and tennis was the least of what I learned from him. He let me borrow books from his library and insisted on discussing them. Blunt in his preferences, he was no literary scholar, but he was smart and relished debate. Sometimes his argumentativeness made me wonder why I put up with him. Was it because he was wealthy and generous? Or because he took an interest in me and my work? When Random House, after six months, still hadn't reached a decision, Philip advised me to shoot off a telegram: "Yes or no on *Man in* Motion?" By return telegram there came a cryptic reply: "Hope terms acceptable. Letter follows." It took ten interminable days for the letter to reach me, offering a fifteen-hundred-dollar advance and informing me that my first novel wouldn't be published for eighteen months.

After such agonizing anticipation, I felt badly let down. The advance seemed paltry, the delayed publication date punitive. But Philip talked sense to me, saying that at the age of twenty-six, time was on my side, and reminding me that the most important point was to get the book into print.

Unfortunately, Philip didn't limit himself to literary advice and tennis tips. He felt free to comment on my social miscues. Once when Linda and I spent a long stay at Montclair, he asked why we hadn't tipped the maid who cleaned the villa. Surely, he said, a hundred francs wouldn't break us.

Humiliated, I blurted out that I had never had a maid and knew nothing about such grace notes. He apologized, then inquired, "How poor were you growing up?"

"How rich were you growing up?" I shot back. "I bet you had maids and nannies and servants."

"Yes, I had all that. But I'm interested in you, Mike. I'd like to know more about your childhood."

"Don't you realize you're embarrassing me?"

"Sorry. I don't mean to. I'm just fascinated by how far you've come."

"You make me sound like a monkey with a typewriter banging out the complete works of Shakespeare."

"Don't take it like that. I'm honestly interested in how you became what you are."

"Ditto," I said.

Later our paths crossed in London, and to show us the kind of life he had led as a child, Philip invited Linda and me to his father's home and introduced us to Sir Robert Mayer, then nearly ninety (he would survive to one hundred and five and be profiled in *The New Yorker*). He showed us the family art collection, which included canvases by Vlaminck and Kokoschka, then treated us to lunch at the Athenaeum Club.

In return, Philip said he wanted to meet my mother and get a firsthand glimpse of where I grew up. This struck me as a very bad idea. I didn't trust how Mom might react. Still, Philip insisted that turnabout was fair play. So I gave him her number, and the next time he was in the States he called and asked whether he could stop by.

"Hell, no," Mom snapped.

I told him not to take it personally. There had been times—and there would be more in the future—when my mother wouldn't open her door to me either. Philip professed to find this, as he did many other aspects of my life, "fascinating." Unlike Professor Henry Higgins, whose focus had been Eliza Doolittle's education, not her grotty past, Philip took an interest in what I had been as well as what he imagined I could become.

Nowadays, this all strikes me as nothing short of miraculous. At a point when I was confused and lost, Philip extended a hand. Later, when I achieved a measure of success, he was delighted and encouraged me to go on. No one else except Linda had ever shown such a personal interest and made such an emotional investment in me. How could I not love him?

It's astonishing the run of good luck I enjoyed back when I was too plagued by doubts and financial difficulties to appreciate it. Now I see that every setback ultimately turned to my advantage. If I hadn't rented that hellish apartment in the Latin Quarter, if I had never made a fool of myself in that French bank, then smashed my fist through a Métro window, I might never have left Paris. And if I hadn't been so financially strapped that I couldn't afford anything except an icy cottage that first winter in Auribeau, I would never have met Philip Mayer. And without Philip, I would never have become passionate about tennis and proceeded to write four books about the game. And if Philip hadn't bestowed Montclair on us, I would never have been able to return to Auribeau year after year and gotten to know Graham Greene.

IV

~~~~~~~~~~

WHEN THE FULBRIGHT ended, I stayed on in Europe, traveling in a frenzy, like a man checking off places on his bucket list. Linda and I drove through Spain and Portugal, then into Morocco as far south as the Sahara. After a summer in England, we traveled to Italy and Greece and over to Egypt, which had severed diplomatic relations with the United States after the Seven-Day War.

As Greene wrote, there are thrills to be had in such troubled destinations as long as you have a return ticket. Our thrills doubled when we flew out of Egypt on Air Algérie, bound for Beirut. At Baalbek, in the Beqaa Valley, Palestinian gunmen skulked around the Roman ruins.

Turkish Air offered a tempting itinerary from Beirut to Rome via Istanbul. We laid over, eating our meals at the Pudding Shop, a cult hangout on the overland route to India where hippies smoked dope and pondered the road ahead. I was tempted to go with them to the end of the line. I wanted to reach a point from which there was no turning back.

But turn back I did and accepted a tenure track position at

the University of Massachusetts Amherst. I had warned Linda that with luck I'd wind up teaching creative writing. But I didn't feel lucky. I felt trapped. All the traveling seemed to have systematically deranged my senses.

Then an attractive alternative presented itself. Larry McMurtry reviewed *Man in Motion* for the *Washington Post* and nominated me for a Wallace Stegner Award. The catch was that Stegner fellows had to spend two years in Palo Alto, at Stanford University. Any sane young writer would count this as a privilege, not an imposition, but I longed to return to Europe. A priest in Amherst said that he knew Graham Greene and now corresponded with him. I wasn't subtle about it—I asked for Greene's address and kept pressing for it until I got it, and realized Greene lived half an hour from Auribeau. It seemed a karmic sign. I quit UMass and declined the Wallace Stegner Award. Then as soon as we settled again at Montclair, I wrote Greene a letter:

> I have long been an admirer of your work, and in recent years our paths have crossed repeatedly, although we have not met. My wife and I lived for a while at the Oloffson in Port-au-Prince, then for a winter in the south of France. In Haiti we missed you by several months; in the south of France I was unable to find an address for you. Now I would very much like to meet you.
>
> I don't suppose it will affect your decision, but I am a young American novelist and a Catholic who envies your technical competence, your energy and your theological probing. Though I wouldn't—and certainly no one else would—compare my work to yours, I feel I have been influenced a great deal by your writing.

I'm stunned now by how stilted this sounds, how stuffed with faint praise. "Your technical competence, your energy . . . and your theological probing" captures nothing of what I felt for Graham Greene. I worshipped the man, but was reluctant to say so for fear of sounding like a sycophant or a stalker.

Within days, a small, square, pale blue envelope arrived. It bore a British postmark but no return address. For the next twenty years, Greene's correspondence always came in this kind of envelope. Greene faithfully answered more than two thousand letters a year, and for convenience he dictated them onto tapes that he dispatched to England to be typed by his secretary.

Dear Mr. Mewshaw,

Thank you for your friendly letter of Aug. 19, [1971].
I'm afraid it would be quite impossible to meet you in Paris
or the South of France as I am leaving for South America
at the beginning of September.

Only somebody as besotted as I was would fail to see this as a brush-off. Months later, like a mechanical bird programmed to sing the same song, I wrote Greene again, adding that I was "anxious to dispel the notion that I'm another 'Waterbury' [an obnoxious character in *The End of the Affair*]. I'm not a newsman, an interviewer, a graduate student or any other type of literary leech. I simply admire your work and would like to meet you."

To my astonishment, Greene replied, inviting Linda and me to his apartment for drinks. Swearing me to secrecy, he revealed his phone number and instructed me to call to fix a day and time. For the rest of his life, whenever I rang, Greene answered by barking, "Who is this?" He never said hello or how are you. The serrated blade of suspicion didn't disappear until he heard my name.

He lived at Résidence des Fleurs on Avenue Pasteur, near the Antibes train station, not, he stressed, on snooty, upscale Cap d'Antibes. His high-rise apartment overlooked the port, indistinguishable from adjoining buildings except for the name Green—the final "e" conspicuously absent—listed on the intercom.

From an antiseptic lobby, an equally antiseptic elevator of buffed aluminum lifted Linda and me to the fourth floor, where Graham Greene greeted us with a stiff handshake. Dupuytren's contracture had frozen a couple of fingers on his right hand. His left, nonwriting hand was fully flexible after an operation. Because it would have meant missing work during rehab, he had refused to have surgery on his right hand.

He was then sixty-eight and a world historical figure. I was twenty-nine, and my initial impression was of a very old man, fragile, stoop-shouldered, with oysterish blue eyes that avoided mine. He was six foot two, an inch taller than I am, but appeared spindly beneath loose-fitting trousers and an untucked floral shirt. The Italian writer Mario Soldati, a friend of Greene's, described him as having "a hurt, offended face, metaphorically bruised by events." Still, he retained an aura—or was this just my jangled nerves?—that made him imposing.

Linda and I were late. I apologized that we had hit heavy traffic after visiting an exhibition of Nicolas de Staël's paintings.

"There's where he killed himself." Greene led us through a flat not much more elaborate than the sort of short-term lets that Linda and I often rented. He gestured in the general direction of the balcony, and beyond it, the ramparts of Antibes: "It doesn't look high enough, but it worked."

That the first words out of Greene's mouth were of suicide struck me as perfectly fitting.

Below us the streets streamed with cars, the noise of horns so loud we had difficulty hearing each other. Greene lamented that the racket kept up long after he went to bed. Because everybody in the building barbecued on their balconies, the smell of seared meat insinuated itself into his sleep. "The world is a raucous radio held to the ear," he had written.

When we moved back inside, it hit me again how meager the apartment was—just a living room, a work space, a bedroom, a tiny kitchen and bath. Malcolm Muggeridge remarked in his memoir, *The Infernal Grove*, that Greene "had this facility for seeming always to be in lodgings and living from hand to mouth. Spiritually and even physically he is one of nature's displaced persons."

He had the reputation of being close-mouthed and secretive. But that night he was gregarious and outgoing. He showed us a painting by the Cuban expressionist René Portocarrero, a gift from Fidel Castro. Castro had autographed the canvas beside the artist's signature.

Although I meant to listen closely and notice everything and forget nothing, Greene's talk shot off on tangents and was difficult to follow. Every anecdote was blurred with pronouns that lacked antecedents and the names of people and places he didn't bother to identify. I half-caught a story about a rendezvous in Cuba with a rebel intermediary who convinced him to smuggle warm clothes to Castro's troops in the Sierra Mestre. After Castro ousted the dictator Fulgencio Batista, he rewarded Greene with the canvas by Portocarrero—or so I understood it.

The topic turned to Haiti. Linda mentioned our honeymoon at the Hotel Oloffson and the meeting with Aubelin Jolicoeur.

"A scoundrel and a spy," Greene declared. "An amusing man, Jolicoeur, but somebody to be wary of."

"Oh, I was wary," Linda said. "He liked to dance and rub up against me."

Greene clapped a hand to his lips and giggled. Then he stepped close to a wall lined with books. Among his novels were copies of books from his childhood and a number of stories for kids that he had coauthored with Dorothy Glover, his mistress during the 1940s. When I asked about his favorite contemporary authors, he mentioned his good friend and fellow Catholic Evelyn Waugh. Then he praised the Indian novelist R. K. Narayan, whose work he had recommended to English publishers.

After a brief search, he found what he was looking for—a bilingual pamphlet entitled *Graham Greene démasqué* (*Finally Exposed*). Published at Papa Doc Duvalier's expense, it savaged *The Comedians* and accused Greene of being a racist, a pervert, and a spy.

Greene was proud to be Papa Doc's enemy. How could anyone accuse him of racism, he asked, when he had Black relatives in the Caribbean?

Greene poured us glasses of Scotch and Perrier. "Pubs in England are so stingy," he said. "Even when you pay for a double, it's never enough."

Alcohol increased Greene's volubility. Or perhaps our questions about Vietnam sparked his growing animation. I thought I recognized the symptoms of mania. Once Greene started talking, he couldn't stop. It seemed his reputation for remoteness had been self-protection. Behind a mask of detachment, he concealed a loquacious nature. Yvonne Cloetta, his mistress for more than thirty years, maintained, "Apart from his writing, he did not live a solitary life in the least. In actual fact, he had a terrible time trying to preserve his solitude."

Greene claimed his memories of Saigon remained so vivid, he had no desire to revisit Vietnam. With a description drawn almost verbatim from his introduction to a reprint of *The Quiet American*, he captured the spell of Southeast Asia. This was a penchant he shared with other novelists, this tendency to paraphrase his published work when recounting personal experiences. He spoke of elegant women in white silk trousers; paddy fields with water buffaloes like primeval statues; opium dens in Chalon. He gave an imitation of Ngo Dinh Diem's hysterical high-pitched laugh and dismissed as nonsense the U.S. government's official denial of involvement in Diem's assassination.

Linda and I had been with him for two hours and had had nothing to eat since lunch. Although he kept our glasses full, he never served hors d'oeuvres, neither that night nor any other time we visited him. When I excused myself to use the WC, I was woozy from hunger as well as Scotch. In the bathroom a kitschy clockwork boat rocked on a ceramic sea, adding to my tipsiness. On the wall hung a notice from the Belize government alerting citizens how to react in the event of a hurricane.

Back in the living room, Linda was listening to Greene describe his first face-to-face encounter with Ho Chi Minh. He said he had felt ill beforehand and feared he might have to cancel the interview. But after a few pipes of opium, he regained his equilibrium. He wrote that opium tended to affect him "like the first sight of a beautiful woman with whom one realizes that a relationship is possible."

By Greene's account, the opium-smoking ritual sounded quasi-religious. Maybe that appealed to him as much as the pleasure of a pipe—the sacramental aspects of the ceremony; the couch and pillow that the smoker reclined on; the ball of brown gum that bubbled over the flame; the dreamy disappearance of anxiety and unhappiness; the twenty-minute doze that felt like it lasted all night.

Unprompted, he brought up his mistress, Yvonne Cloetta, whom he met in Duala, Cameroon, when he was returning from the Congo, where he had spent weeks researching *A Burnt-Out* Case in a leper colony. He had gone there feeling like a burnt-out case himself. But falling in love with a thirty-six-year-old married Frenchwoman had revitalized him. She moved with her two children to Juan-les-Pins near Greene, leaving her husband, Jacques, behind in Africa.

According to Greene, they saw each other every day. He worked in the morning and kept at it until midday. Then Yvonne arrived for lunch. Afterward, he said, they took "a little nap."

His readiness to disclose his private life to complete strangers surprised me. He sounded less like a buttoned-up British novelist with an Oxbridge accent than an over-sharing Californian. Just as freely as he had described the opium-smoking ritual, he volunteered information about his affair.

Yvonne was still married to Jacques Cloetta and her cuckolded husband flew back from Africa every summer to spend a long holiday with his wife and family. During these annual visits, Greene traveled. He swore the arrangement worked for them and he added with a grin that Jacques was Swiss—as if that explained everything. Greene suggested Jacques was either unaware or didn't care that his wife was sleeping with another man. He showed not the slightest twinge of sympathy for Jacques, nor any sign of his famous Catholic guilt and remorse.

This wasn't what I expected. But then biographer Michael Sheldon emphasized in *The Enemy Within* that Graham Greene was an expert at frustrating expectations. "He liked to make villains sympathetic, innocent characters guilty, heroes weak. He found beauty in ugly settings and ugliness in the most attractive places. He wrote novels disguised as thrillers, created religious tales full of doubt and a love story filled with hate."

On a coffee table in the center of the room, several maquettes were displayed. Linda picked up a miniature sculpture of an abstract reclining nude, a sinuous ensemble of metal curves and lacunae. It had been a gift from Henry Moore, Greene said, worth fifty thousand pounds.

Linda picked up a second piece, a chrome-plated, vaguely phallic cylinder a foot tall. She hazarded a guess that it was by Brancusi or Jean Arp.

"I have no idea," Greene said. "I bought it from a chemist in Nice. What you'd call a pharmacist."

"Didn't it come with papers about its provenance?"

"The papers it came with," Greene drawled, "recommended using it twice a day in the event of itching or inflammation. I suffer from hemorrhoids. It's a medicine applicator. It's so decorative, I couldn't bear to keep it in a cabinet." As a memorable remark this ranked right up there with Harold Robbins's wisecrack about having his eardrums punctured.

Linda daintily set it down and resisted what had to have been an overpowering impulse to wipe her fingers on Graham Greene's shirt. Was this a joke? A cruel prank? A bit of fun with a pair of greenhorns? A test of how far he could trespass?

Or was it payback after spilling intimacies about Yvonne and her husband?

Greene's better self resurfaced as Linda and I stood up to leave. He said he'd like to see us again. He promised to phone when he returned from a trip to Spain. Meanwhile, he wanted me to have a signed copy of one of his books in exchange for my second novel, *Waking Slow*, which I had sent him.

Craning his neck to check the shelves behind him, he said, "Here's an edition of *The Quiet American* that Penguin never released." A one-of-a-kind mock-up, it featured a hand-painted hardback cover glued to a paperback. Greene scrawled an inscription that I didn't look at until we were in the elevator. Light-headed from hunger and Scotch and the unfathomable events of the evening, I burst into laughter. Small spidery letters spelled out "In exchange for *Walking Slow*. Affectionately Graham Greene."

The misspelled title seemed a perfect kiss-off. Neither of us believed we'd ever see Graham Greene again.

V

⬦⬦⬦⬦⬦

B<small>UT A COUPLE</small> of weeks later, Greene did call as promised, and proposed "giving" Linda and me dinner in Mougins. That's how he always put it—not inviting us to dinner or treating us to dinner, but "giving" us a meal.

"The only problem is transport," Greene said. "I don't drive."

I was gobsmacked. The restless explorer of the wildest bends and elbows of the Third World, the adventurer I longed to emulate, couldn't convey himself a dozen miles from Antibes to Mougins. Buses covered that route, and there were cabs for hire. But brave and confident as Greene was in the jungle and on the battlefield, he had vast areas of incompetence. According to his sister, he couldn't even change a lightbulb; he'd rather call an electrician. Paul Theroux noted in the *New York Times* that Greene "could not cook, he was incapable of using a typewriter, he did not wield a map; he was a naturally dependent not to say helpless man . . . we can easily understand his need for a lover."

I confess that I share some of Greene's fumble-bum defects. I'm a non-typing novelist, a non-cooking gourmand, an inveterate shirker of domestic chores, inept with almost every mechanical and electronic device. But I do drive. So I happily chauffeured Greene to Mougins over twisting country roads redolent of night-blooming jasmine into hills then devoted to agriculture, not investment properties.

Long-legged and ungainly, Greene hunched beside me in the passenger seat, squinting through the windshield at cars rushing toward the coast. He was reluctant to buckle his seat belt, perhaps because it would wrinkle his loose-hanging shirt. Or maybe because he hated feeling tied down.

"Dreadful, this traffic," he said. Because he had trouble pronouncing the letter "r," this came out "Dwedful, this twaffic."

"I don't mind it," I said. "I love to drive. I have ever since I was a teenager."

"I prefer to fly."

"I'm afraid of flying."

"He's absolutely terrified," Linda chipped in from the back seat. "He has to take twenty milligrams of Valium for a two-hour flight."

"Why do you worry?" Greene asked. "At least when your plane crashes you're not crippled for life. You die."

I laughed. "That's what scares me—dying!"

"I'd rather be dead than mangled."

With the evening off to a woeful start, I tried to lighten the conversation. I asked why he had settled in Antibes, assuming he'd talk about Yvonne Cloetta. Instead he glumly replied, "Death duties."

"Excuse me?"

"I needed to escape English death duties." He meant inheritance taxes, not the threat of capital punishment. During the sixties, a corrupt money manager had bilked Greene out of a large share of his wealth. To recoup his losses and provide for his heirs, he became a tax exile.

Like me, attempting to find a lighter topic, Linda mentioned she had read that American journalists assigned to Vietnam competed to rent his apartment in Saigon.

"I never lived in an apartment," Greene said. "I stayed at the Hotel Continental." It amused him that gullible American reporters were so easily swindled. "They deserved to get gypped. So much of what they write about Vietnam is tripe."

IN HIGH SUMMER, Mougins heaved with tourists divided into two distinct camps—those who looked like celebrities and those looking for celebrities. The parking lots outside the town walls resembled luxury car showrooms, packed with Porsches, Maseratis, and Ferraris. At times the line of people pressing to get through the village gate grew so long, nonresidents without confirmed hotel or restaurant reservations were turned away.

Picasso lived nearby and knockoffs of his ceramics and bullfight posters were bestsellers in dozens of souvenir shops. The Moulin de Mougins boasted three Michelin stars, and the central square was surrounded by restaurants that aspired to that culinary status. Lately the town had attracted an influx of film stars and directors, both foreign and French. Yet nobody appeared to recognize Graham Greene, one of the twentieth century's most respected movie critics and screenwriters. Bypassing posher restaurants, he led us to an unprepossessing establishment that offered shepherd's pie, a humble plate of minced meat under a crust of mashed potatoes. Greene told us it was his favorite dish.

As we ate our pub grub, washed down with a very good Médoc red, the talk turned, as it often did with Greene, to Vietnam. Richard Nixon promised to end the war "with honor." But Greene had no illusions that U.S. troops would soon come home, or that the current South Vietnamese regime would survive without American aid. He remembered the French endgame in 1954 at Dien Bien Phu and the catastrophic decision to commit twelve battalions of soldiers to the defense of a hopeless position. Rather than concede defeat, French politicians prolonged the butchery for fifty-seven days. "Hasn't the Pentagon learned anything from history?" Greene asked.

In every war, he said, his sympathy lay with the victims. He naturally empathized with the colonized Vietnamese, who lost twenty-three thousand men at Dien Bien Phu. At the same time, he acknowledged his feelings for the twenty-two hundred French soldiers who had needlessly died there. Far more American troops, he predicted, would perish for a mistake.

Greene described how Vietnam had introduced him to "the great American dream which was to bedevil affairs in the East." Washington was obsessed with locating, or creating if necessary, a Third Force as a bulwark between the Communists and the corrupt Saigon regime. The CIA deluded itself, he said, that the Caodaists constituted such a force.

A modern syncretic religion that combined elements of Confucianism, Taoism, Buddhism. and Roman Catholicism, Caodaism revered a wacky pantheon of saints including Julius Caesar, Joan of Arc, Victor Hugo, and Sun Yat-sen. The Americans didn't mind. All they cared about was that the Caodaists controlled an army of twenty thousand men. "They were capable of causing trouble," Greene explained, "but didn't have the power to achieve a solution."

While he discussed the big picture and long-range geo-political objectives, Greene didn't give short shrift to specific painful incidents he had witnessed. He recalled a battle at Phat Diem, describing the "neatness" of the bullet holes in a mother and little boy floating dead in a canal. I was reminded of the kid I couldn't save from drowning in the creek across from my house. If that horror plagued me after twenty years, how many more memories must have tormented Greene? As a novelist he hadn't just imagined bloody traumas. He had lived them and came away with emotional scars.

When the waiter brought the check, Greene produced a wad of French francs fastened together by a straight pin. I asked Greene about Edwin Lansdale, an infamous U.S. Air Force officer who had transferred to the CIA and coordinated the outreach to the Caodaists. "Was he the model for Pyle in *The Quiet American*?"

"No, Lansdale didn't show up in Saigon until after I had finished the novel," Greene said. He tweezed out the pin and handed the waiter two hundred francs. Then he stitched his money back together. "Anyway, I conceived of Pyle as an innocent. Whatever else you can say about Lansdale, he was no innocent."

"Was there a model for Pyle?" Linda asked.

"All fictional characters are composites," he said. "A straight roman à clef doesn't interest me. It doesn't leave room for the imagination. I prefer to invent. But there was a minor American diplomat in Saigon. I seduced his wife and decided that Pyle must be the same sort of Boy Scout as her husband."

To WALK OFF our dinner, we strolled around town with crowds of other *flâneurs*. In Place du Commandant Lamy, a bearded, uniformed statue of the nineteenth-century military hero stood like a rebuke to the casually dressed pedestrians. Because I was preparing to write *The Toll*, a novel set in North Africa, I knew a bit about illustrious French officers who had made their reputation in the Sahara. Like Lamy, many of them had adopted the tactics of the local tribes, surviving on a diet of six dates a day and fighting pitched battles on camel-back. Lamy died near Lake Chad, during a campaign against a Sudanese warlord. "But he was born and raised here in Mougins," Greene said. "His house is on one of these streets."

We entered a maze of alleys lit by lamps that glazed the cobblestones silver. "What's a *wap*?" Greene asked. The word sounded like a wet rag splatting on concrete. Neither Linda nor I had a clue.

"James Baldwin wang me last week from Saint-Paul-de-Vence and said he and Margaret Mead had published *A Wap on Wace*. Now he suggested doing a wap on weeligion with me."

"A 'rap' is slang for a talk, a lively conversation," I said.

"I think I'll let Baldwin wap alone," Greene said. "I'm at the point where I loathe discussing weeligion. I'm always misquoted."

We paused in front of Commandant Lamy's birthplace, which had a plaque above the door. Weeds sprouted between the pale stones of the porch. No one appeared to have visited in a long time.

"I'm enjoying your novel." Greene spoke as if this were his purpose in bringing us here—to praise *Waking Slow* in privacy. He added that he was impressed by the Los Angeles setting and found the book very funny. Then without drawing a breath, he itemized the things he didn't like. The plot revolved around a love affair between a pregnant coed and an earnest Catholic boy who helps her put another man's baby up for adoption. In short, it revolved around *me*, and so it smarted when Greene objected to the sex scenes. He especially disliked the terms "tits" and "panties." As we started back to the square, he suggested I substitute "knickers" for "panties." Neither of us thought to consult Linda about women's lingerie.

Disappointed to have Greene veer from applauding *Waking Slow* to cataloging its faults, I almost regretted giving him a copy. Reviews in the States had been few in number and negative enough to leave bruises. Now Greene was re-opening old wounds.

But then in the car en route to Antibes, he asked permission to show *Waking Slow* to Max Reinhart, his editor at the Bodley Head. He advised me that he couldn't guarantee anything. Reinhart didn't always agree with Greene. Still, he felt that the book deserved to appear in a British edition.

In a thank-you note the next day, I wrote how much Linda and I had enjoyed the evening in Mougins: "What pleased us much more than the ample drink and abundant food was your cordiality." We invited him to Montclair for dinner before his departure for Spain during Yvonne's annual reunion with Jacques Cloetta. But then Philip Mayer returned early from Ireland and we had to move temporarily into our original cottage in Auribeau, the one with the hallmarks of Le Corbusier's style.

In summer I could appreciate that the house might be mistaken for "a machine for living." But during our renewed tenure, death stalked the kitchen. Or rather, Linda and I stalked a family of field mice that had nested under the sink. We baited traps and tensely awaited the *clack!* that signaled another furry corpse needed to be discarded. The task fell to me. Sympathetic toward the baby mice we slaughtered, Linda opted out of burial duty.

The evening of the dinner with Graham Greene, I fetched him from Antibes, and because the round-trip took an hour, I dreaded how many guillotined mice might pile up in my absence. Naturally I was nervous. Who wouldn't be with Graham Greene coming to dinner and the kitchen crawling with mice? I tried to make small talk, mentioning we were having difficulty deciding where to spend the fall.

"Why not Brighton?" Greene suggested. In *Ways of Escape* he had written that "no city . . . not London, Paris or Oxford had such a hold on my affections." But his depiction in *Brighton Rock* suggested anything except affection. With its shingle beach as penitential as a bed of nails, its British sunbathers laid out like bodies in a morgue, it was the perfect setting for a murder mystery in the form of a morality play.

"We're looking for somewhere warm," I said. "Someplace where we can play tennis."

"Brighton's often quite mild in autumn, and it has tennis courts. Of course there's the rain."

"We're considering Spain. The Costa del Sol."

"That'll be expensive," Greene argued. "In England, tennis is a middle-class sport. In Spain, it's a rich man's game. Don't you find it distasteful that you'll be lining General Franco's Fascist pockets with cash?"

I considered and quickly dismissed the temptation to tease him that his upcoming excursion to Spain would also support the dictator. I told him we had found a flat in Marbella at a bargain price.

"If it's cheap, it's bound to be appalling," Greene said.

LINDA WELCOMED US in Auribeau, her eyes moist with tears. Maybe Greene mistook this for delight at seeing him. She whispered that I'd better tend to business in the kitchen. Under the sink, the smallest mouse yet, hairless and pink, lay broken in a trap like a barbecued shrimp on a grill.

Resetting the trap, I joined Linda and Greene. Dry-eyed now, she had poured him a whiskey and listened to him praise Brighton. I kept an ear cocked for the *clack!* of another execution.

By the time we sat down for the first course—a tomato salad with diced onions in vinaigrette—no trap had sprung, but I remained rigid with anticipation. Greene too appeared tense. Painstakingly, he separated the tomatoes from the onions. He nibbled bread that he dunked into the vinaigrette, avoiding the tomatoes altogether.

Linda looked distraught. This probably struck Greene as regret at her failed first course. I knew better and hearing a *clack!* I hurried into the kitchen to tend the traps.

The second course was roast beef and *pommes de terre au gratin*. "I apologize for the meat," Linda said. "I'm afraid I've overcooked it."

"One gets sick of raw beef in France," Greene reassured her. "This is delicious."

Between bites, we discussed American authors. Greene observed that they reminded him of what Churchill had said about Russia: "They're a riddle wrapped in a mystery inside an enigma. I find them very strange. Why do they all feel compelled to marry every woman they sleep with? I've been married to the same woman since 1927. Think of Norman Mailer and Saul Bellow and all their wives. Think of the alimony they must pay. A staggering amount."

He sliced his beef into bite-size slivers that he pushed with his knife onto the back of his fork. "Some writers seem to have the mark of Cain on them," he said. "Malraux has that facial tic, and Sartre has a walleye and Moravia limps and Steinbeck's got a terrible complexion. Maybe Mailer's curse is that he can't stop marrying."

Like clockwork, a mousetrap sounded. "Time for dessert," I said. After I discarded the fresh carcass, I brought *mousse au chocolat* to the table. Greene pronounced it "Marvelous" and ate a second helping topped with whipped cream.

ON THE ROAD back to Antibes, I drove slowly and cautiously. I had had too much to drink. Greene had also had a healthy share of alcohol and spoke with a slight lisp, as he often did when he overindulged. "I apologize for upsetting Linda," he said, "by not eating the tomatoes."

"She probably assumes you have an allergy."

"It's a bit more embarrassing than that." He explained that as a young man he feared he had contracted what he called a social disease: "I consulted a doctor and he told me never to eat tomatoes. I've obeyed his instructions ever since."

I laughed, thinking this was Greene's tipsy attempt at humor. But he insisted he was serious and cited his recent introduction to a reprint of *Brighton Rock* that referred to the social disease and the doctor's advice. I didn't have it in me to correct Greene; Linda was crying over dead mice, not uneaten tomatoes.

The Great Man's idiosyncrasies and odd beliefs didn't reduce him in my estimation. They humanized him, made him more accessible, raised my respect for what he had accomplished. No less than Malraux, with his nervous tic, and Sartre, with his walleye, he was an author who had triumphed over innate awkwardness to create great art.

VI

◇◇◇◇◇◇◇◇

FOR A PERSON of depressive tendencies, autumn can cause killing sadness. My mother used to collapse every year at the first whiff of wood smoke. Like Margaret who in Gerard Manley Hopkins's poem is "grieving / over Goldengrove un-leaving," I too suffered sorrow as summer ended. There was a seasonal sense of loss, of being downsized, as we departed from Montclair. I always worried that Philip wouldn't ask us back.

With Graham Greene I suffered similar insecurities. He had thousands of readers and admirers. How did I differ from the hordes of importuning authors who hunted him down begging for literary help? In *Congo Journal* he expressed bewilderment: "Why should this dream of writing haunt so many? The desire for money? I doubt it. The desire for a vocation when they find themselves in a life they haven't really chosen? The same despairing instinct that drives some people to desire rather than experience a religious faith?"

How awful it must have been for Greene, a man often troubled himself, to be badgered by broken people who saw him as their salvation. It embarrassed me to imagine that he might view me in that category. To prove otherwise, I could of course have left him in peace. Instead I chose to believe that I understood him and had something to offer. I could listen and talk to him, I could amuse him and make him laugh. I presumed that because I knew his books, I knew the man, and that this lifted me above his legions of other acolytes. He had written, "I'm not a genius. I'm a craftsman who writes books at the cost of long and painful labour." Surely if I worked as hard as he did and displayed the same depth of commitment, he'd recognize me as a kindred spirit.

On route to Marbella, Linda and I checked for mail at American Express in Madrid. To my consternation, there was a letter from my agent in London boasting that she had sold the British rights of *Waking Slow* to Constable. There was also news from the Bodley Head that they wanted to publish the novel; Graham Greene's recommendation had persuaded Max Reinhart. Appalled, I telegrammed Greene to apologize and explain that *Waking Slow* was already under contract.

He might well have accused me of wasting his time and dismissed me as an ingrate. Instead he sent congratulations and urged me "to do some editing on the lines I suggested . . . I do think you should control the tits and panties! They get in the way of those splendid characters Eddie and Fingerhut." He also sent a blurb for Constable to use in publicity: "Mewshaw has a remarkable sense of place. One of the best black comedies I have read in many years."

Along with a letter of thanks to Greene, I enclosed a copy of *Love in the Ruins*, by Walker Percy: "I thought his ideas about Catholicism might interest you. Somehow he's managed to become very popular in America in the last few years."

Greene replied that the Percy novel was "a bit long. I class it high in the ranks of those books which one reads once for pleasure but one is unlikely to reread." His letter ended: "I'd very much like to see you and Linda again."

After six weeks in Marbella I wrote, "The Costa del Sol seems to resemble the Côte d'Azur in August. The streets are clotted with bars. The traffic noises are thunderous, and tour groups have infested every nook and cranny. Perhaps several Spaniards still live somewhere within a dozen miles of the Mediterranean, but I haven't seen them. One can walk for miles along the shore and never hear anything except German, Swedish, or English."

Linda and I left Spain earlier than planned and after spending a month in London returned to the States, traveling to Los Angeles, Austin, and New Orleans. As I told Greene, "My reaction to maps and the names of places is almost Pavlovian. I always want to pack up and leave."

I didn't write him again until we had settled for the winter in Key West, what I called a "small spit of land off the tip of Florida. Not a bad spot really since most tourists don't get down this far, perhaps because the beaches are bad. But the weather and vegetation are wonderful, and the old part of the town has a shabby charm that suits us fine."

In fact, Key West in those days was nearly derelict, and apart from sailors at a U.S. Naval base, the population consisted mostly of shrimpers and drug runners and homosexuals searching for a tolerant home. Bare-bones Bahamian houses sagged against each other like skeletons in a catacomb; roosters, herding harems of hens, commandeered the sidewalks. It would be decades before cagey investors gentrified the island into a replica of Provincetown. Linda and I lived in a renovated rooming house on Caroline Street along with two gay couples and a disapproving widow who swore she had nothing against homosexuals except for their rampant promiscuity and lack of fervor for Jesus Christ.

I wrote Greene:

We both read and enjoyed *Travels with My Aunt* . . . We also saw the movie . . . Then [we] visited the University of Texas which we were delighted to learn had your papers and manuscripts. We spent an enjoyable day thumbing through them . . . Auden said that literature is the best way of breaking bread with the dead. We discovered that it's also a good way to break bread with the absent.

Yet I hope our dealings won't continue to be indirect. There's a chance we may be returning to Europe and the South of France late this spring. It depends largely upon whether I'm able to arrange to do an article on the Cannes Film Festival.

Near my thirtieth birthday, in February 1973, Greene answered:

Your tip of Florida sounds attractive even to me. I'm all for shabby charm. I gather from another visitor to the University of Texas that while you examine the papers you are watched by internal television and there are men with guns at every door.

After three years I at last finished that novel which was giving me such a bad time. It's called *The Honorary Consul* and is being published this September. The Book of the Month Club have taken it as their full September choice which is at any rate good for my publisher's purse who gave me much too big an advance . . . I do hope you manage to come for the Cannes film festival and I hope still more that I shall be around—not for the festival but to see the two of you . . .

I haven't seen the film of *My Aunt* but from all accounts I certainly don't want to. In that case it will be the second of my films I've managed to avoid. The first was [John] Ford's travesty of *The Power and the Glory* under the title of *The Fugitive*. [George] Cukor [who directed *My Aunt*], seems to belong to the travestiers, though I would have expected him to be closer to the transvestites.

I enlivened my next letter to Greene with a scarcely believable tale that had the virtue of being entirely true:

Key West has lost a bit of its charm for us. Shabby it still is. Seedy it now seems. Last Saturday night or Sunday morning I woke from uneasy sleep to find a stranger standing beside my bed, no more than a foot from my face. He was reaching for my wristwatch on the nightstand. With infinite calmness and presence of mind, I levitated ten inches and let out a primal shriek. The burglar, perhaps more frightened than I, screamed back and dropped his banana. Yes, his banana. It seems he was carrying a big black mushy one instead of a pistol. At least I assume he had the piece of fruit for that purpose. Anything kinkier sends shudders up my spine.

At any rate, I screamed, he screamed and ran for the door, and Linda and I raced him to it. He won, and as his reward he fell down the front steps. I was barefoot and in my underwear and couldn't catch him. Actually, I wasn't awake even then. Full consciousness didn't occur until a few minutes later when I discovered that he had been in our apartment for some time, carefully going through Linda's purse and my wallet. He hit us for $50, and the next door neighbors for $300. The cops came about half an hour later and put on a Laurel and Hardy routine. When I asked whether they intended to dust for fingerprints, they acted as if I had suggested they use an astrologer in their investigation. Though we weren't resigned, they obviously were, and told us quite blandly—as if this would set our minds at ease—that it was probably just a drug addict. Needless to say, we've now nailed our screens shut and have bought big locks and chains for the door. Sleep has become a precious commodity. We nod off for a few minutes every few days. Mostly we just wonder what would have happened if our friend had had a gun instead of a banana.

Greene answered:

I liked very much your fruity story. I have intercepted twice the same man trying to open the door of my neighbor in these flats. I think he's deranged rather than a robber, but that is hardly more encouraging. As a result I bought in Rue de la Paix a teargas bomb which I keep handy.

On the same day that he wrote me, Greene sent a sympathy note to Gillian Sutro, whose husband, John, had suffered a breakdown. The world, he said, seemed racked by absurdity. For instance, "A young writer in Florida wrote to say he had been held up at the point of a black banana by a robber in his own house." This wasn't, strictly speaking, how I had described the incident to Greene. There had been no banana-point confrontation with the thief. I wasn't aware then of Greene's penchant for embroidering events.

ON THE CHANCE that we might miss each other in Antibes, Greene wrote to give me a "very secret phone number" and suggested, "Maybe you'll look in on Capri on your travels. Unless [Yvonne and I] happen to be making an excursion we shall always be found at the Villa Rosario in Anacapri. It's at the very far end of Anacapri in the district known as Caprile and the people will know where it is. Nearly always we take a drink in the piazza of Capri between 7 and 8 and have dinner at Gemma's so you shouldn't find any difficulty in locating us."

Greene had schooled me well that he went to Capri "to have peace and to work" and to be alone with a woman he loved. He insisted he never rented the villa and seldom allowed family and friends to use it. In her concise pointillist memoir, *Greene on Capri*, Shirley Hazzard recalled with affection, nicely balanced by astringent candor, the evenings she and her husband, the literary scholar Francis Steegmuller, had spent with Graham and Yvonne. But Greene's recollections were a lot less nostalgic. He told me that he found Hazzard's pressure to socialize and trade intellectual gossip tiresome and oppressive. He lamented that she had almost ruined the island for him.

So, flattered though I was by the suggestion, I never considered dropping in on Greene on Capri. If he could grow weary of Hazzard and Steegmuller, I didn't delude myself that he couldn't tire of my company. But I once went to Anacapri alone in winter and easily found the Villa El Rosario on Via Caselle. A small place formed by two buildings that had been joined together, the villa had the vaulted-roof architecture seen everywhere in North Africa—white as dice, adorned with dark windows like pips on each side.

WHEN I SUCCEEDED in scoring press credentials for the Cannes Film Festival, Linda and I enjoyed a sunny week in the dark, watching a crop of new movies. Then in the evening we swanned around at cocktail parties with Carlos Saura, Jerry Schatzberg, Lina Wertmüller, and John Frankenheimer, the last two of whom I later worked with.

After the festival we met Graham Greene for lunch at Chez Félix au Port. The owner seated us outside at a protected table where we didn't need to worry about our napkins blowing away in the wind. I recounted my interview with Dominique Sanda, who had originally been cast opposite Marlon Brando in *Last Tango in Paris*. She swore she hadn't been disappointed to lose the role to Maria Schneider. "I was pregnant and didn't have the body Bertolucci was looking for," she told me. "I was happier to have my baby than the role."

"But wouldn't it have been wonderful," Greene exclaimed, "to have her in *Last Tango*? Did you see her in *The Conformist* and *The Garden of the Finzi-Continis*? Her delicacy would have been such a terrific contrast to Brando's brutality. Maria Schneider looked too much like a match for him."

Ages before the advent of the #MeToo movement, Greene had no reluctance to rate women on the basis of their looks. He had recently eaten dinner with François Truffaut and Jacqueline Bisset, and he raved about Bisset's beauty and desirability.

He didn't just grade and objectify movie stars. He had an eye for attractive women whenever and wherever they crossed his path. In one of two journals written in Africa, *In Search of a Character*, he noted the "third best-looking" woman he had encountered.

As a film reviewer, however, he was never swayed by surface glamour. A keen critic, he took movies seriously as art, yet never so seriously that he suppressed his wit. Between 1935 and 1940, he did more than four hundred reviews for the *Spectator* and *Night and Day*, and his description of Mae West should have been chiseled on her tombstone—"the Edwardian bust, the piled peroxided hair, the seductive and reeling motions reminiscent of an overfed python."

Even Shirley Temple, America's child sweetheart, didn't escape his wicked sarcasm. He accused 20th Century–Fox of showcasing her "oddly precocious body as voluptuous in grey flannel trousers as Miss Dietrich's" and implied that her song-and-dance routines appealed expressly to leering pedophiles. This provoked Fox to file suit for libel, forcing *Night and Day* out of business and nearly bankrupting Greene.

Undeterred, he went on to an illustrious screenwriting career—sometimes adapting his own works, sometimes creating original scripts. *Brighton Rock*, *The Fallen Idol*, *Loser Takes All*, *The Third Man*—these and many more remain lasting movie landmarks.

That day at lunch Greene maintained he still followed the movies, but his filmgoing sounded as sporadic as his attendance at Mass. While his youthful devotion had faded, a few remnants of the old faith remained. He said he had liked David Bowie's *The Man Who Fell to Earth* and encouraged us to see it.

The University of Texas had recently hired me to set up a creative writing program. This entailed moving to Austin, a not altogether attractive prospect, in my opinion. But it prompted Greene to inform us he had cofounded, along with the British movie producer John Sutro, the Anglo-Texan Society, the madcap product of a day of drinking in the bar of Edinburgh's Caledonian Hotel in the company of two lovely young ladies from the Lone Star State. After more drinking on the train back to London, the men drafted a letter to the *Times* announcing the society's birth and declaring Greene president and Sutro vice president. Membership was free and open to the public.

In 1954, the society threw a party to commemorate Texas's independence from Mexico. Fifteen hundred guests gathered at Denham Film Studios and polished off almost three thousand pounds of barbecued beef and countless barrels of cider. Although Greene resigned his presidency on April Fool's Day 1955, the society lived on and still hosted events. Greene hoped I would join.

The lunch at Chez Félix au Port ended with coffee and a recap of our travel plans. Linda and I intended to drive down the Dalmatian Coast and catch a plane from Athens to Egypt, where I hoped to set my next novel—if another Arab–Israeli war didn't preempt the plot.

Greene was headed to the opposite end of the continent. *Playboy* had hired him to do an article about South Africa. He admitted misgivings about the magazine, but said he was eager to judge for himself how likely Blacks were to rise in violent rebellion against apartheid.

This struck me as an impressive excursion for a man approaching his seventieth birthday. But Greene claimed he wasn't worried and added that he had no preconceived notions. While all right-thinking people regarded South Africa as a pariah state and decried its racism and savage repression, he pointed out that Western nations, for all their posturing, actually feared it would fall under Black rule or, worse, under Communism. The self-appointed Children of Light protested apartheid, Greene said, but secretly counted on the Children of Darkness to do their dirty work, protecting the region's mineral wealth and its strategic position between the Atlantic and Indian Oceans.

He acknowledged another reason for accepting the *Playboy* assignment. His current novel—one that he had laid aside years ago and only recently picked up again—dealt with a white British Intelligence agent in South Africa who marries a Black woman and returns to London as a paper-pushing, deskbound spy. Entitled *The Human Factor*, it had originated in Greene's determination to show the reality of espionage, which, he said, involved humdrum bureaucracy rather than car chases, sexual sprees, and bloody assassinations.

"I put the book away," Greene went on, "when the Kim Philby business blew up. There are similarities between my plot and the Philby affair and I didn't want anyone to think I had drawn on that. There has already been enough nonsense about my friendship with Philby. Perhaps now the novel can be read on its own terms."

His link to Kim Philby went back to 1943, when both men worked for British Intelligence. For Greene, joining the SIS amounted to entering the family firm. His sister and brother-in-law had recruited him; several other relatives also had connections with espionage.

Philby was operating under diplomatic cover when he first met Greene, and the two of them shared a love of drink and literary banter. Unbeknownst to Greene, or to British Intelligence, Philby was by then already a double agent, one of the infamous Cambridge Five, who passed information along to their Russian handlers. When Greene's wartime posting in West Africa ended, he briefly served under Philby in London, monitoring Portuguese counterespionage. Outside the office, they were social acquaintances, nothing more.

Before WWII ended, Greene resigned from the SIS, claiming he preferred to return to writing novels, not filing memoranda. Later, he amplified that explanation and insisted he had started to view Philby as a careerist and a social climber; Greene said he didn't care to be a cog in the man's rise as an Establishment insider. Philby's version of events was markedly different. He argued that he had let Greene go to avoid involving him in a hall-of-mirrors life.

The truth of the matter remains a subject of debate. Was Greene a pawn in ongoing espionage? Had he been at any point a double agent? After Philby's defection to Moscow, in 1963, questions about the two men proliferated. Some suspected that they exchanged coded messages. Others speculated that Philby was actually a triple agent and that Greene was his conduit for feeding information about Russia to the U.K. After the fall of the Berlin Wall and the advent of perestroika, Greene paid Philby several visits in Moscow, then passed on reports to British intelligence. Was he double-crossing Philby? Was he disseminating bogus or genuine intelligence to the Home Office?

In a long life of secretiveness that began at Berkhamsted School, Greene's relationship with Kim Philby represents another unresolved enigma. According to Father Leopoldo Duran, his Spanish friend and deathbed confessor, Greene was troubled till the very end of his life by his involvement with British Intelligence.

WHEN PHILIP MAYER discovered I had become friends with Graham Greene, he didn't conceal his disapproval. For Philip, all religious belief was illogical, only a notch above black magic. But it wasn't Greene's or my Catholicism that nettled him. He loathed Greene's politics, particularly his left-wing sympathies and his assertion that, if forced, he'd rather live in the U.S.S.R. than the United States.

Philip had traveled widely throughout Russia and its satellite states, and had reported on the U.S.S.R.'s ethnic persecutions and programmatic torture. He predicted that the Soviet Union would eventually implode under the weight of its internal contradictions. No system, regardless of how repressive, could survive, he said, when it ignored human nature and economic reality.

I avoided arguing with Philip. His distaste for Greene reminded me too much of the treacherous position I had occupied between my divorced parents. In this instance, I felt torn between two surrogate fathers. Living in one man's house and the other man's reflected glory, I was afraid that the slightest disloyalty to either of them would leave me out in the cold. I wasn't about to take sides—even though I knew Greene had written "One has to take sides—if one is to remain human."

Philip Mayer considered Kim Philby a traitor, a murderer who had sentenced his own men to death by unmasking them to Moscow. He accused Greene of being not only a passive fellow traveler, but an active accomplice in Philby's crimes as well.

He bought me a copy of Philby's *My Secret War* and urged me to read Greene's introduction before I decided whether I wanted to have anything more to do with the man.

Like Greene's fiction, the introduction crackled with irony and paradox and perverse Jesuitical reasoning. It set up strained comparisons and contrasts and false equivalences. Greene described Philby as having "a sharp tooth of the icicle in the heart"—which might sound damning to anybody ignorant of Greene's conviction that ice in the heart was a necessary quality for a novelist.

He defined modern intelligence as mostly "psychological warfare . . . the main objective is to sow mistrust between allies in the enemy camp . . . The West suffered more from Philby's flight [to Moscow], than from his espionage." His defection had humiliated England and delivered a serious blow to the nation's reputation for excellence in intelligence, a source of pride for a country in military and financial decline. It had undermined forever the illusion of the U.K. playing the role of Greece to America's Rome, of a wise old nation educating a young naive one in the dark arts of statecraft.

Rather than dispute that Kim Philby had betrayed England, Greene demanded, "Who among us has not committed treason to something or someone more important than a country?" This echoed E. M. Forster's controversial quote: "If I had to choose between betraying my country and betraying my friend, I hope I should have the guts to betray my country." There hovered over Greene's question an allusion to his own history of infidelity, of his cheating on his wife with prostitutes and lovers, then cheating on his mistresses with other lovers.

Against the charge that Philby had sent men to their death, Greene parried, "So does any military commander, but at least

the cannon fodder of the espionage war are all volunteers"—
unlike infantry conscripts, who are given no choice.

At the height of the Cold War, Greene dared to compare
Philby's Communism with his own conversion to Catholicism.
Both required leaps of faith; both the Church and the political movement, he conceded, were flawed systems. In Greene's
estimation, Philby possessed "the logical fanaticism of a man
who, having found a faith, is not going to lose it because of the
injustices or cruelties inflicted by erring human instruments."

Like the whisky priest in *The Power and the Glory*, Philby
had stayed the course and kept the faith. Despite the evils of
Stalinism, he refused to join the chorus of fallen-away apostles
who cried out "God is dead" when it was the system, not the
deity, that had failed.

When this introduction defending Kim Philby appeared,
in 1968, it sparked outrage. Literary scholars speculated that
it had cost Greene the Nobel Prize. Even his ardent support-
ers objected to the essay's flippant tone and its mean tweaking
of bourgeois noses. Critics protested that Greene had lost his
moral compass and had substituted political sophistry for the
morality of his fiction. Where was the engagé author who had
refused the Malaparte Prize because of Curzio Malaparte's fas-
cism or who later resigned from the American Academy and
Institute of Arts and Letters to protest the Vietnam War?

I confess I never asked Greene these questions, just as I
never challenged his flexible Catholicism or his flagrant infi-
delities or his casual cruelty, or his slippery grasp of the truth.
None of this would matter until things backfired on me.

VII

<small>⋄⋄⋄⋄⋄⋄⋄⋄⋄⋄⋄</small>

F OR THE SIX years we had been married, Linda and I
seldom had a fixed address. For the past two years, we
hadn't resided anywhere longer than three months at a stretch.
So settling in Texas figured to be a culture shock. But I never
imagined how rocky our arrival in Austin would be. The president of the university welcomed new faculty members with
a catfish fry on a pseudo–Mississippi riverboat that churned
through the turbid waters of Lake Austin. The temperature at
six p.m. was ninety-five degrees and the Lone Star Beer on tap
we drank barely moistened the batter-fried fish.

We rented a house outside of town in the Hill Country.
The owner insisted on reclaiming the place every summer,
which was fine by us. We figured we'd be in Europe during
those months.

Meanwhile, it wasn't unpleasant to spend time with fellow
members of the writing faculty. The Pakistani novelist Zu-
lfikar Ghose and his Brazilian wife, Elena, cooked pungent
curry dinners and served potent gin drinks. When we got together with them and the English poet Christopher Middleton

and the Canadian poet David Wevill, there was a suggestion in the heat and semitropical foliage of India during the raj. As the temperature cooled at nightfall, tarantulas the size of a man's hand stepped daintily onto the lawn and took leisurely strolls. Herds of free-range deer, no more frightened of humans than were the tarantulas, ambled through the cedar breaks. After dinner, the leftovers were stuffed into barrels and sealed with rubber straps to frustrate the bands of frisky raccoons.

Upon the publication of *The Honorary Consul*, I wrote to Graham Greene with praise:

> Your usual skilled handling of setting, style and construction brought us the usual pleasure, but we appreciated even more the humor and poignancy of Charley Fortnum, and the sad pomposity of Saavedra. For my money the scene where Saavedra refuses to sign Dr. Plarr's letter was one of the best in the book . . . Though you satirized Saavedra and writers like him, you didn't deny him his humanity, and the following scene, when he offers himself as a hostage, re-emphasizes what is best about him.

As for our acclimation to Austin, I wisecracked, "How are you going to keep them satisfied with catfish after they've tasted turbot?" I added, "We are consumed with curiosity about your trip to South Africa. Maybe you don't want to talk the subject to death before you finish your article for *Playboy*."

Greene answered:

> I went to South Africa but not with the help of *Playboy* as they sent me a contract which would have given them the right to demand that I altered my article or tried to alter it

in accordance with the wishes of the editor. I sent them a telegram to put it up you know where. I went however to South Africa on my own and found it on the whole rather boring—neither as bad as I had expected nor as good as one never hoped. Lovely scenery of course but scenery can become monotonous after three hours of driving through the same hills and colours. I doubt if I'll write anything about it. The impression I came away with is the only hope for South Africa and for the Africans in South Africa were the Afrikaans. The English are too delighted to have several servants to look after them, although the English language press is very independent and very good. But then so are some of the Afrikaans [sic] papers. There is a big liberal movement among the Afrikaans [sic] and it's only from them that I think any hope can come.

Interestingly, a recent biography of Graham Greene, *The Unquiet Englishman*, mentions nothing about a contractual dispute with *Playboy*. Instead, the book maintains that the magazine had wanted Greene to track down and profile the mercenary Mike Hoare. A pairing of Greene, the famous adventurer, with Hoare, the infamous gun for hire, must have struck Hugh Hefner as better value than a geopolitical report. But apparently Hoare was in the Far East, "pursuing murderous business opportunities."

On the advice of friends, Greene declined to travel to the Angolan war zone, which bristled with land mines. A rendezvous with Mangosuthu Buthelezi, the ruler of KwaZulu, who was considered a political alternative to Nelson Mandela, fell through. Apart from visits to several Black homelands, Greene mostly restricted himself to the company of Afrikaner authors and intellectuals. Then, beset by lumbago, he was laid up in the hospital.

Flying back to Paris "exhausted and miserable," as *The Unquiet Englishman* put it, Greene gave an interview to the *Telegraph*, which quoted him claiming he had "been dragged about 2,000 miles in four weeks." He complained about not being able to carry out independent research. Under the circumstances, he told the *Telegraph*, he didn't feel qualified to write about South Africa. There was no mention of *Playboy* magazine, much less of an assignment to write about Michael Hoare.

This wasn't the first or the last time that Greene's correspondence with me contradicted what he reported to others or what his biographers wrote. It didn't occur to me until much later that he might have had his reasons for adopting a different persona with me than he did with others. Perhaps he assumed that I'd be impressed—which I was—by his brusqueness with editors and magazines and his blasé attitude toward prominent people and unstable places. But this caused problems when our versions of events conflicted.

To my praise of *The Honorary Consul*, Greene replied:

Reviews of the new book have been fairly good on both sides of the Atlantic, but one gets tired of a book when once it's written and one gets tired of reading reviews which recount the story." Writing to another friend, his tone was altogether more exuberant. *The Honorary Consul* "seems to me to be about my best. I was getting tired of having to say that *The Power and the Glory* was the best—published in 1940.

He ended by telling me that he "[looked] forward to seeing your new novel [*The Toll*] sans tits sans panties! Don't ever let an editor do it to you again. All editors in America begin to imagine themselves as a kind of Maxwell Perkins but none of them are. Thank God I'm too old for them to try their tricks on me!"

In what quickly became an annoying pattern, people asked me to intercede with Graham Greene. Douglas Day, my dissertation director at UVA, had written a biography of Malcolm Lowry and he urged me to make sure that Greene read the galleys. Better yet, that he blurb them.

At least I knew Douglas Day. In fact, we had become close friends, and he was a crucial source of support for my fiction. More to the point, I could vouch for his talent. (The biography of Lowry went on to win the National Book Award.) I can't say the same for numerous editors and agents, press and TV reporters, all total strangers, who urged me to act as intermediary.

Then, in a separate category, there were the entreaties from the Humanities Research Center at the University of Texas. Within weeks of joining the faculty, I was press-ganged into serving as a middleman. On October 10, 1973, I relayed a message asking Greene:

Would you be interested in coming to the University for a symposium in your honor. They would take that opportunity to display your manuscripts and, I suspect, display you as well. I told the [HRC] . . . that I doubted you'd be interested in coming to America, much less to Austin, Texas.

But if the idea of the symposium somehow stirs you, just say the word. Of course Linda and I would love to see you. But all things being equal I think I'd rather be in Antibes, or as W. C. Fields had carved on his tombstone, I'd even rather be in Philadelphia.

I took this opportunity to tell Greene that Paul Bowles had called *The Toll* one of the most convincing books he had ever read about Morocco. I added that I was trying not to worry about the novel's reception. "My goal is to emulate your detachment. But then maybe that's won only after many more battles than I've been through."

Then I wrote:

It was just announced that Spiro Agnew has resigned. I guess this means that his cries of innocence and his declarations that he would never step down are now 'inoperative.' My hope is that Nixon will fall, too, by the end of November, so that we can all look back on the last decade and think with pride that we have somehow managed as a country to lose two presidents, one vice president, two presidential candidates, one Supreme Court Justice, several civil rights leaders, a war, and any number of minor things like international prestige, financial security, and domestic progress through killing, assassination, avarice, and absolute ignorance. In the entire history of the world it would be difficult to find such a decade in which all this devastating damage was not done by foreign enemies or invaders, but by ourselves to ourselves.

GREENE WAS NORMALLY a punctual correspondent. When months passed without an answer, I worried something had happened to him. As classes at Texas broke for Christmas, and Linda and I drove to California for the holidays, we stopped along the way in Arizona at the San Xavier del Bac Mission and bought stationery at the gift shop. Each card bore a hand-cut print of the church façade festooned with decorative devices done by natives of the Sonoran Desert in the eighteenth century. I knew the combination of a whitewashed adobe church and tribal designs would please Greene more than a sled and reindeer in the snow. Like me, he detested traditional Noel sentimentality.

While we cruised through the red-rock desert, I dictated Season's Greetings to Greene, which Linda transcribed on the new stationery in her flawless calligraphy.

> Due to the energy crisis, there are almost no cars on the road which unrolls before us straight as a plumb line . . . It's a weird way to spend Christmas, I guess, but better than the alternatives.

It wasn't until we returned to Austin, in mid-January, that I discovered that Greene had written to me on New Year's Eve:

> This is a rather shame-faced letter. I did get the proofs of your new novel and eventually I got to the novel itself. I ought to have written to you a long time ago, but I was embarrassed because frankly I didn't like the new book. I found the sex passages unconvincing with that sort of day-dream quality which one finds in Hemingway's accounts

of fucking. I had a feeling that the umbilical cord had not been completely cut.

Sex played a minimal part in *The Toll*, just as "tits" and "panties" hadn't figured much in *Waking Slow*. I found it strange that Greene seemed so squeamish. Given his multiple affairs and his fixations with brothels and sex shows, I wouldn't have expected him to object to a novel that was far from X-rated. *The Toll*'s plot revolves around a jailbreak in Morocco that goes catastrophically wrong. If it is guilty of any sort of prurience, it is of hardcore violence.

My first break with autobiographical fiction, the novel meant an enormous amount to me, and I had hoped it would appeal to Greene. Set deep in Greeneland, it was a story of action as well as ideas, and like much of Greene's work, it threaded the personal with the political. Although I realized it was unwise to respond to criticism, I couldn't resist writing back.

Though of course I wish you had liked *The Toll*, I appreciate your candor. And please don't let your reaction to anything I write prevent you from keeping in touch with us.

Obviously, in the new novel, I was cutting very close to some Hemingwayesque clichés. Rather than be coy or evasive about it, I decided to play right into the teeth of the matter by choosing the title which I did, selecting an epigram from *For Whom the Bell Tolls*, insisting that the publisher mention Hemingway in the flap copy, and giving the characters names similar to the ones in *For Whom the Bell Tolls*. (Puff = Pilar, Polo = Pablo, Ants = Anselmo, Gypsy = Gypsy.) There are also any number of incidents and themes which may at first blush seem to have been lifted [from Hemingway]. But what I have tried to do in each case is summon up in the reader a certain expectation, and then thwart that expectation and hopefully force him to re-think his initial assumption. I meant for the sex scenes—of which there are exactly three—to remind the reader of Hemingway's adolescent wet dreams, but I wanted him to be aware of the differences between Robert Jordan and Maria's relationship and Ted and Bert's. At the start Ted isn't interested in her, and she is playing him along to get his help. Never are they completely open and honest, and from the middle of the book on, they not only have no sex, they have very little communication, and the two of them quickly deteriorate emotionally and physically to the point where there is no possibility of their staying together. Whereas Robert Jordan is dying but tells Maria they will be together always, Ted and Bert survive but realize that because of what has happened—what Ted has been forced to do—they'll always be separated. More than anything it was my intention to show that Hemingway's facile assumptions about politics, military action, and human relations are intrinsically American and by extension were at the root of a great deal of our difficulty in Vietnam, among other places.

Please excuse me for running on like this. The book is what counts, I realize. If you don't reach the reader there, you don't deserve to reiterate your intentions in a letter, telegram, or smoke signal. But I wanted you to know that I was aware of the Hemingway influence. Maybe, as you suggested, I just wasn't able to cut the umbilical cord completely.

Ironically enough I just received word that the Bodley Head [Greene's publisher] has outbid Constable for the British rights to *The Toll*. They paid me a very fine advance, and have already sold the paperback rights to Quartet . . . My editor will be James Michie. Do you know him?

As I often did after speaking my piece, I felt compelled to conclude on a lighter note:

I sympathize with your uneasiness about dental surgery. I've always detested the dentist and still avoid him as much as possible. But maybe Ajax Menekrates [Greene's wonderfully named oral surgeon] has one of those high-speed, air-cooled drills, and all of the other awesome equipment that reduces the discomfort to a minimum. And of course as Sister Catherina used to say to me in the seventh grade, you can offer it up for the repose of the souls in Purgatory. That never made me less frightened, but I had a feeling that my fear and pain were putting wings and haloes on my grandparents. A reassuring thought.

Greene answered:

Thank you so much for your letter and for not taking offense at mine! I'm delighted that the Bodley Head are doing the book. James Michie is a very intelligent man and a good poet. His translations of Horace's *Odes* with the Latin on one side and his verse translations on the other was a remarkable effort.

I'm having a rather dreary time spending about 4½ hours a week with Ajax—uncomfortable and tiring rather

than painful. It looks like going on until May. What makes
me want to scurry back to my desk if only I had a single
idea is the price—£5,000! I don't believe it would cost more
in the States.

Again, I tried to cheer him up:

I've just been reading Evelyn Waugh's *Scoop* and thought
you might be interested in hearing the following anecdote.
Just after the recent publication of *The Toll* I was asked
to appear on a local television program. The interviewer,
of course, had not read my book, or any other book for
that matter, and so after a wandering conversation about
the weather, the vagaries of literary life, and the dangers of drinking and drugs, there was little to talk about.
Made uneasy by the silence, the woman began to study the
back of my book, then suddenly looked up eagerly, having gotten an idea. "Whatever gave you the idea that you
as a white man could understand the Negro problem in
America? Aren't you running the risk of being accused of
exploitation?"

Stunned, I managed to mumble, "What?"

"It says right here on the back of the book, 'One of the
best black comedies I have read in years.' What makes you
or Mr. Greene (pronounced Green-ey) think a white man
can understand the black situation? And what's funny
about it, anyhow?"

Foolishly I tried to explain what black comedy was.
She didn't believe me. Or maybe she just didn't care, since
that was more literary than controversial. Only after I had
staggered off the stage did I realize I should've taken her

up on the issue she raised. It would've been much better for me to pretend my book was about the black problem. I'm told there's nothing like being publicly attacked to build up sales. But I wasn't nimble-witted enough to know this.

Greene replied, "What a wonderful story. You can see what I escape by my refusing to appear on television under any circumstances."

OUR TENTATIVE PLAN had been to return to France in June 1974. But in mid-August, I let Greene know that events—some foolish, some fortunate—had conspired against us:

First, for the foolish—in late May David Susskind optioned the film rights to *The Toll*. Soon afterward another producer became interested in my work and wanted me to come to Hollywood for the summer to write an original screenplay. He wouldn't tell me much about the project on the telephone, which should have been my first warning. So Linda and I drove to the West Coast only to find out that the producer wanted me to do a script for a high-budget science fiction movie about people who turn into fish. Seems the man [Douglas Trumbull] who did the special effects for [Kubrik's] *2001* had invented a new technique for underwater photography, and they're just dying to use it. All they needed was a vehicle, i.e. a script. I declined on the grounds that the whole thing sounded absurd . . . Actually I was frightened off by the prospect of doing dialogue for fish.

When we reached the East Coast," I continued, "we still had intentions of coming to France, but Linda didn't feel well. In fact she seemed to have come down with some sort of lingering malady. Finally she went to the doctor who assured her the illness wasn't fatal, although she had contracted it from me. According to the doctor, we should be parents sometime next March. Of course I'm deeply pleased, but at the moment it doesn't seem a very likely prospect. It'll take a few more months, I guess, for Linda to grow and for the idea to grow on me.

What with David Susskind optioning the film rights [to *The Toll*] and an unexpected shower of gold from a federal government agency called the National Endowment for the Arts, I believe I can take off from teaching for the next few years. It remains for me only to finish out the coming school year in Texas, complete my new novel—a religious comedy which will probably sell 16 copies—and wait for Linda to recover from the baby.

Greene greeted the news:

All good wishes to all three of you. Your venture to the West Coast and your retreat is worth a short story." As for his own work, he sounded despondent. He was ghosting "the memoirs of a colorful female doctor who had led a chaotic life on Capri." He described the woman as "a combination of Chaucer's Good Wife of Bath and Mrs. [Molly] Bloom." Apart from that, he lamented, he had "no ideas at all for anything at present. More than a year has passed without any real work except stray autobiographical articles which the *Daily Telegraph Magazine* are publishing. [These would later appear in book form as *Ways of Escape*.] Perhaps the desire to write will return in time.

WHILE I WAS busy teaching, book-reviewing for *Texas Month-ly* and the *New York Times*, editing student short stories, and accompanying Linda to natural childbirth classes, the desire to write fiction was what sustained me. That and the equally keen desire to engineer an escape to Europe. Linda had started looking at real estate in Austin and I feared that if we bought a house I'd be lost. I'd become another harried husband, in hock up to my eyeballs, pushing a baby carriage around campus, checking out each year's new crop of coeds.

Not that I wanted out of my marriage or ever considered leaving Linda. What I wanted was to discover a solution that allowed us both to be happy. What I wanted was a way of living that didn't leave me as disconnected and adrift as Graham Greene sometimes appeared to feel. It didn't dawn on Greene or me that incessant travel was hardly a cure for disconnection and drift.

Because France was expensive and its laws finicky about foreigners overstaying their visas, Italy seemed a better place to establish a temporary base. Robert Penn Warren and his wife, Eleanor Clark, recommended that I apply to the American Academy in Rome, which accepted me as a visiting artist. In the academy's hierarchy, this allowed me access to an office, to the library, to conferences and panel discussions, and to the dining room. Because Linda and I would be arriving with a baby, we couldn't live in the main McKim-White building, but we were provided with what was described as "a functional apartment" nearby. That sounded dreadful, but the academy had a red clay tennis court and that clinched the deal for me.

Despite my apparent impulsiveness, I was careful not to burn bridges with the University of Texas. Rather than resign, I took the first of what became semiannual leaves of absence.

We landed in Rome with our six-month-old son, Sean, who flew overnight in a cardboard box. Instantly I was spellbound by the city—not a reaction original to me. As Henry James, more than a century ago, had written, "No one who has loved as Rome could be loved in youth wants to stop loving her."

My attraction was less to the sublime classical ruins and architectural splendors than to the appealing mayhem of contemporary life. Rome abided by no rules. Even the laws of gravity seemed suspended. Traffic lights and pedestrian zones signaled safety only to the deluded and the soon-to-be dead. A local brand of cigarettes bore a label in the shape and color of a stop sign, implying that when Italians see *STOP!*, they naturally Go!

Without visas or residence permits, we existed entirely off the books. We paid no taxes, never opened a bank account, always settled our bills in cash, and drove a borrowed car that belonged to an art historian who hadn't bothered to update its Dutch tourist plates for a decade. In that era, when urban terrorism was rampant and the Red Brigades lurked in safe houses all around Rome, I thought of myself as hiding in plain sight, like a secret agent in a Graham Greene thriller.

We got to know people ranging from belligerent landladies to benevolent parking lot attendants, Nobel Prize-winning authors, and hacks who churned out English subtitles for Italian films. The pick of the litter, my best friend in Rome, was Donald Stewart, a former staff writer at the *New Yorker*, who now edited *Playboy International*. When he heard that I knew

Graham Greene, he contacted his bosses in Chicago and they invited me to do a profile based on my evenings with Greene in Antibes. They offered fifteen hundred dollars on acceptance— the same as the advance for my first novel. If the article was rejected, I'd still get a three-hundred-dollar kill fee—a tidy sum compared to the seventy-five bucks the *New York Times* paid for book reviews.

The money meant less to me than the opportunity to express my admiration for Greene and remind readers of his central position in the contemporary canon. Still, I had misgivings about the assignment after Greene described his tiff with *Playboy* over the article on South Africa. Then, too, I was acutely aware of my paltry journalistic experience and regretted that *Playboy* refused to cover my expenses to revisit Greene and refresh my memory. But then *Playboy* declined to pay any expenses. I'd have to depend on my notes and the correspondence we had exchanged, as well as on Linda's recollections.

My greatest fear wasn't rejection by *Playboy* but giving offense to Greene. I wrote to him in December 1975:

> I was trying to get in touch with you last month. I called Antibes several times, then rang the Bodley Head. They took my name, number, and address and, I trust, passed along the news that *Playboy* has asked me to do an article on you. I don't know about the protocol of these things, but I wanted you to know what I was doing. Needless to say, it's a very positive article and I hope it presents a picture which is true and interesting and informative. What I did basically was re-create the first meeting of ours several summers ago, allowing you to speak in your own voice about your work habits, travels, experiences, etc.

Of course there's no guarantee that *Playboy* will publish it. I haven't done many articles and may well botch this up. I'll be sure to let you know their response.

Linda, Sean, and I spent Christmas 1975 in Paris, then caught a train back to Rome after New Year's. We planned to stop for a couple of days in Cannes, I told Greene, and he could read a typescript of my article then, if he liked. Greene wrote:

> I haven't known that you were trying to get in touch with me. They never passed along the information. This was probably because I had just lost my secretary and things were in a bit of a confusion. I confess I feel a little nervous about the *Playboy* article. I hope you don't give away any secrets of my private life!

The train trip from Paris with an exuberant nine-month-old proved far more exhausting than anticipated. If I hadn't promised to show Greene a copy of the *Playboy* article, I would have swallowed my fear and flown the family to Rome.

Linda begged off the lunch in Antibes, and I joined Greene at Chez Félix au Port, where on a bright chilly day he sat at an outdoor table beside a tiny woman who had a helmet of short silver hair. Pretty and perfectly groomed, Yvonne Cloetta, then fifty-one, looked much younger than her age and had a pert, gamine air. Like Greene, she had blue eyes, but hers sparkled while his were pale with age.

Yvonne owned a dog named Sandy that Graham cuddled in his lap. The Golden Spaniel was much better behaved, I thought, than Sean had been on the train. When Yvonne left the table for the ladies' room, the dog docilely followed her.

While she was gone, Greene begged me not to include her in the *Playboy* article. I swore that I wouldn't, and since I had brought a draft of the piece with me, he could check for himself. He brushed off the suggestion; the day was too beautiful to waste time reading about himself.

If the good weather held, he and Yvonne planned to cross the Italian border to the Ligurian Riviera. Portofino figured to be blessedly free of crowds now that the holidays were over. I recommended a hike over the hills to Camogli, a village just as beautiful as Portofino but less tarted up for tourists.

When Yvonne returned, she had freshened her makeup. Because she was attractive and almost two decades Greene's junior, one might mistake her for mere eye candy, an old man's arm ornament. His pet name for her was HHK, short for Healthy Happy Kitten.

But I soon learned how crucial she was to him both personally and professionally. She was his companion, his cook and chauffeur, and because by his own admission Greene spoke execrable French, she served as his translator and his go-between with French editors and the French press. Unlike Greene, she also spoke Italian, which came in handy on Capri.

More significant, she kept a diary that would prove invaluable to future scholars and biographers. In addition to recording names and dates and places, she jotted down notes about Greene's moods and troubled emotions, especially his angry outbursts. She didn't shy away from showing him at his worst. In her memoir, *In Search of a Beginning*, she described him in a rage at a three-star Michelin restaurant, Fouquet's Paris, smashing an ashtray. Periodically, Greene read her journal, with Yvonne's permission, and added in the margins his comments and corrections, some quite extensive.

After lunch, over coffee, we discussed the situation in North Africa, which appeared to interest Yvonne more than it did Greene. When I told them I intended to travel to Tunisia, then down through Algeria to the Sahara, she was anxious about whether Linda and the baby would be with me. Once we established that I'd be alone, she was relieved.

Before we parted company, Greene caught me off guard, saying that he continued to mull over the invitation to fly to Texas and inspect his archive at the HRC. He might visit as early as next spring. He recalled passing through the state decades ago, en route to Mexico for *The Lawless Roads*. While researching that book, he had been reading Trollope's *Barchester Towers*, he said, lighter fare than *The Anatomy of Melancholy*, which he had lugged through the sweltering jungle when doing *Journey Without Maps*. He said he had fond memories of San Antonio, and wondered whether someone from UT could drive him there. And how would the university react if he arrived with Yvonne?

FOR THE FOLLOWING two years, we discussed and rediscussed his potential trip to Texas. This provided a diversion from the fate of my article: *Playboy* had turned it down, complaining that it sounded less like a profile than an adulatory valentine from a young writer to an older one. Word reached me via Donald Stewart that editors in Chicago were disappointed that my piece contained few personal disclosures. Didn't Greene have a mistress?

Greene was relieved that *Playboy* refused the piece. But I was embarrassed and believed that I had failed him. I urged my agent, Owen Laster, at William Morris, to submit it to other magazines.

As rejections rolled in, I kept up a positive drumbeat in my correspondence with Greene.

It really would be shame if you didn't go to Texas this spring. I realize I must sound like a member of the local Chamber of Commerce given the way I keep touting the state . . . It's simply that I believe you would enjoy yourself and like many of the people, especially if you could steer clear of all the bores and jerks. Actually I don't know many of the bores and jerks by name, but I'm sure you'll recognize them. The men tend to wear white shoes and loud plaid outfits, and the women have blue rinse hair and flowered dresses. The main thing to keep in mind is that as the honored guest you could quickly establish your own ground rules and insist on seeing what and whom you please.

Since we were in Rome and in no position to welcome him to Austin, I compiled a list of people he should look up, along with brief CVs and home phone numbers for each of them. "If you got the urge to reacquaint yourself with Laredo or to do a little slumming," I wrote, "I'm sure that Bill Wittliff, who has done a filmscript about Boystown [a red-light district on the Mexican border], could arrange a visit."

Greene, who suffered his own bouts of manic behavior, must have recognized mine as I ran off the rails with advice. His answer was short and to the point:

I have more or less decided to go to Texas, though I can't bring myself to bargain for more money. I did drop a hint that traveling first class would about exhaust the honorarium! I find I can go direct from Paris to Houston, but by that time there may be a Concorde to Washington which would be rather fun.

While I negotiated to get his travel allowance beefed up, Greene's plans abruptly changed, and without explanation he canceled the trip. Perhaps in compensation, he wrote to me:

I took *Earthly Bread* away with me to Greece and thoroughly enjoyed it. I think it's your best book. I left the proofs with my brother Hugh and I hope he'll boost it at the Bodley Head.

As Greene's junket to Texas collapsed, I carried through with my journey from Rome to Tunisia and Algeria. Then, after a month in North Africa, I fetched Linda and Sean at the airport in Nice and delivered them to Montclair, which Philip had put at our disposal until August. I finished a rough first draft of *Land Without Shadow*, a novel set in the Sahara, and polished off numerous book reviews to help pay the bills. Our bank balance had dwindled and we were forced to ask overnight guests—at one point fifteen people, including Douglas Day and his mistress, squeezed into the villa with us—to kick in a couple of bucks a day for wine and groceries. Much as I liked to imagine myself as the reincarnation of Gerald Murphy, presiding over the A-list of authors at the Villa America in the 1920s, I was more than normally irascible that summer, vexed by the racket of guests arriving and departing, and guilt-ridden that so much of the social heavy lifting fell to Linda.

A wiser man might have realized that it was time to settle down, buy a house in Austin, and stop frazzling back and forth between the United States and Europe. Instead, an idea started to take root that I should quit teaching altogether and support myself in Rome as a freelance writer.

WE INVITED GREENE to Auribeau for lunch that summer, and this time "transport" presented no problem. Yvonne owned a sporty white Opel. Greene probably envisioned us in the same mouse-haunted house where he had had dinner. When I met him at the gates of Montclair and Yvonne pulled into the broad parking lot of checkerboard flagstones, he looked astonished. With Sandy tucked under his arm like a rugby ball, he stood beside the car in what I had come to regard as his uniform—loose-fitting tan trousers and an untucked shirt in a floral pattern. He gaped in wonder at the massive old *mas*, the seven acres of grounds, the swimming pool, and the tennis court. Compared to the frugality of his apartment, the place was baronial. Incredulous, he asked, "Does it belong to you?"

"No, it belongs to a friend. He lets us live here while he's in Ireland."

Suddenly I didn't know whether to be proud or ashamed to be living in such opulence. Would Greene think worse of me if he believed I was rich? Or even less if he thought I was a moocher? "We look after the upkeep," I said, "and cover the expenses for utilities and the telephone. And there's a maid and a gardener. It comes to hundreds of dollars a month"

"That's nothing for a property like this," Greene spluttered.

"Would you mind showing us around?" Yvonne asked.

As we strolled past the pool to the tennis court, I felt like a hideous hermit crab that inhabited a splendid conch shell. "The owner likes having a permanent tennis partner. That's where I fit in," I tried to explain.

Greene scrutinized Montclair. Or was he scrutinizing and reassessing me? Sandy started to wriggle under his arm as he and Yvonne paused under a tree. Greene called it a linden. Yvonne insisted it was a *tilleul* tree. Its leaves made excellent tea, she added. Meanwhile, I marveled at Graham Greene in the role of dog carrier and amateur horticulturist. Where was the man who once wrote "Nature doesn't really interest me—except in so far as it may contain an ambush."

Yvonne went on ahead to greet Linda, and while Greene and I lingered, I asked if he'd like to take a dip before lunch; he could use my spare swimsuit.

"No, thanks," he said. "Without clothes I'm self-conscious. I have four nipples."

Delivered deadpan, this sounded like one of his outlandish jokes. But who knows? Years later I noticed in his collected letters a reference to this rare affliction—which didn't exclude the possibility that Greene was repeating a punch line.

As Linda called us to the table, Greene told me, "I never rent my house on Capri or my flat in Paris. A place that's lived in by a succession of strangers soon becomes a home to nobody."

I didn't know how to reply. Surely he didn't mean to insult me. Or did he? A character in *The Comedians* remarks: "It was as though somebody I hated spoke from my mouth before I could silence him." That was how Greene sometimes sounded. A friend once described him as "only happy when he was being unhappy." Did he actually suspect me of angling to move into one of his houses?

He grew increasingly petulant during the meal. Perhaps he resented that I hadn't informed him there would be other guests. Two lovely young ladies from Arkansas lavished attention on him. He might have welcomed this if Yvonne hadn't been there.

It struck me again how attractive Yvonne was, a perfect miniature. I couldn't help comparing her to Catherine Walston, whom Greene had considered the love of his life. Where Yvonne was sedate, primly dressed, and silver-haired, Catherine had been dark-haired and given to wearing dungarees and going barefoot at dinner parties. Evelyn Waugh characterized her as "unaffected to the verge of insanity."

Both women were associated in Greene's mind with Africa—Yvonne because they had met in Cameroon; Catherine because . . . It's better to let Greene express it in his own words: "You're my human Africa," he wrote to Catherine. "I love your smell as I love these smells. I love your dark bush as I love the bush here, you change with the light as this place does so that one all the time is loving something different, yet the same. I want to spill myself out into you as I want to die here."

It was inconceivable that Greene would write Yvonne such a letter. He had once brought her to a brothel in Paris for a sex show. It was the sort of thing Catherine and he had done together, with Catherine disguised as a man. Yvonne recoiled in disgust and fled the joint, thinking that Greene intended to arrange a threesome. She put her dainty foot down; she wouldn't abide such sordid behavior.

It was similarly inconceivable that Yvonne shared the intensity—and the strangeness—of Greene's religious obsessions. He and Catherine had attended a Mass said by Padre Pio, a Capuchin monk reputed to suffer from the stigmata. Afterward he and his lover used cigarettes to burn the stigmata on their palms. Greene regarded this as a serious religious experience, not a perversion. He told George Orwell that visiting Padre Pio had "introduced a doubt in my disbelief."

At lunch that day, there was also a literature professor who invited Greene to lecture at his college. Greene declared that he didn't do that kind of thing, ignoring his off-and-on flirtation with the HRC.

When the professor asked about James Joyce, Greene answered that he liked *The Dubliners* but considered *Ulysses* overrated and *Finnegan's Wake* unreadable. As for Virginia Woolf, he disparaged the whole Bloomsbury Group and pointed out that that's why he made Major Scobie's wife in *The Heart of the Matter* an avid Woolf fan. Both the wife and Woolf were insipid, he said.

These kinds of peremptory judgments didn't sit well with academics. Barthes and Derrida then ruled on campus and it was customary for literary assessments to be expressed in impenetrable jargon. Greene, by contrast, shot from the hip, with a gunslinger's disregard for the glittering lights he shot down as collateral damage. When asked to blurb Michael Herr's *Dispatches*, whose excerpts in *Esquire* had already drawn raves, Greene replied to the American editor: "I read *Dispatches* naturally with great interest. I was rather put off by the opening part which seemed to me too excitable, but Herr calmed down a bit later. I think when one is dealing with horrors one should write very coldly. Otherwise it reads like hidden boasting— 'just see what a brave chap I am to have voluntarily put myself in the way of such experiences. To adapt Wordsworth, horror should be remembered in tranquility.'"

Eventually Greene disengaged from the professor and simply sat and stroked Sandy's golden fur. To break the silence, one of the lovely American ladies asked, in all innocence, "Do you run with the English crowd in Nice?"

She might have been Daisy Miller doing her naive best to amuse an aging, grouchy European. But Graham Greene wasn't having it. "I don't run with any crowd," he growled.

The lunch limped to a close, and as I walked them around to Yvonne's car, she praised Linda's cooking and her French. *"Elle parle comme une française."* Then she told Greene that she looked forward to discussing the lunch conversation on the drive home.

"I'd rather have a bullet in the head," he said. Instantly, he added, "Forgive me. This isn't one of my better days."

VIII

∞∞∞∞∞∞∞∞∞∞

WE GOT TOGETHER again that summer before Greene departed for Spain and his annual driving trip with Father Duran and before Linda and I commenced the long trek back to Texas. He was in a far better frame of mind, as he invariably was at the prospect of traveling. At Chez Félix au Port, we had a table in the shade and each of us ordered a glass of cold white wine and lemon sole.

Greene mentioned that he had just appointed a biographer. He downplayed the significance of the decision and denied that at his age, seventy-two, he sensed vultures circling overhead. He understood that with or without his permission, somebody was bound to write his life story. Although he preferred that this occur after his death, he accepted that his control was limited. Still, he refused to relinquish all influence and did what he could to prevent an unqualified person from grabbing the job.

He had admired Norman Sherry's book about Joseph Conrad, he told us, and was impressed by Sherry's determination to follow in Conrad's footsteps around the globe. Because of Conrad's early exile from Poland and his original career as a ship's captain, this had obliged Sherry to undertake a Herculean journey.

If he displayed the same diligence in tracing every obscure path through Greeneland, he didn't figure to finish his research for decades. That prospect filled Greene with malicious glee. "I will live to see your first volume, but not your second," Greene taunted Sherry. "And you will not live to see the third."

In Greene's opinion, Sherry's geographical approach to biography had an added benefit. The more attention he spent on Greene's outward journey, the less he would have to dwell on his subject's interior life, especially his sexual escapades. (To the distress of Greene's survivors and heirs, Sherry dug deep enough to rankle them and damn him as a traitor.)

That sunny day in Antibes, Greene alerted me that Sherry would be in Austin for the fall semester, reviewing the archive at the HRC. Afterward, he would assume a tenured professorship at Trinity University, in San Antonio, an hour's drive south of Austin. Greene urged me to help Sherry, who hailed from Lancaster, England, feel at home—or at least less deracinated—in central Texas.

This raised once again the possibility of Greene's visiting Austin. He said it all depended on his schedule. He liked to reserve spring for a stay on Capri with Yvonne. But this year an unexpected opportunity had arisen. For reasons that Greene had difficulty fathoming, General Omar Torrijos, the dictator of Panama, had invited him, seemingly out of the blue, to fly to Colón as his guest, all expenses paid, including a seat across the Atlantic on the Concorde. Greene claimed to be "mystified" by the opportunity to have this late-in-life adventure, but in fact he had been attempting to arrange it for several years. Enlisting the assistance of the U.S. journalist Bernard Diederich to engineer the visit, serve as translator, and introduce him to important Panamanians, Greene drew on his five trips to Central America to produce several prominent articles, a memoir, and an aborted novel and a published one.

This struck me as a very bad idea. Because of his sympathy with Third World struggles, Greene had always supported "victims," sometimes on the left, sometimes on the right. But this Panamanian junket had the potential to involve Greene in a dubious propaganda campaign for a dangerous regime. I should have saved my breath. Greene soon committed to making the trip to Panama.

Whether this justified his Panamanian junkets and his involvement with some very dicey characters is highly debatable. Although a dictator, Omar Torrijos may have been every bit as intelligent and attractive as Greene portrayed him. (Diederich described Torrijos as "a delightful mad hatter-type modern caudillo.") But surely the same can't be said of Manuel Noriega, the head of Torrijos's intelligence service and later his vicious drug-dealing successor. Reflexively sympathetic to victims of what he perceived as American malfeasance, Greene went so far as to say this: "If I have to choose between a drug dealer and United States imperialism, I prefer the drug dealer."

This was a replay of his remark that he'd prefer to live in Russia than in America. But as a provocation intended to prompt discussion about U.S. foreign policy, it fell flat. It struck many people that for a novelist who had made a career of exploring the theme of betrayal, Greene had now betrayed himself. John le Carré, long an admirer of Greene's, put it more politely, commenting that late in life Greene "tended to confuse his prominence as a novelist with a degree of political standing that he did not really possess."

WHEN WE RETURNED to Austin, Linda and I usually had no trouble renting a house from a professor on sabbatical. In 1976, however, we found nothing we could afford and crashed with the screenwriter Bill Wittliff and his family while we continued searching. Finally we resigned ourselves to a place that belonged to a woman who was on the road most of the week, throwing parties where she peddled the Mary Kay line of cosmetic products. She had divided her house in half, and we rented the part accessible from the front entrance while she used a side door.

Because the place came unfurnished, we leased two mattresses, not beds, just mattresses, plus a crib for Sean, a couple of chairs, and a couch that clashed with the burnt orange, high-shag carpet. (But what wouldn't clash with a burnt orange, high-shag carpet?) As I wrote to Greene, "It was all we could do to keep from turning around and going right back to Europe."

I didn't need to speculate what people made of our—pardon the expression—lifestyle. They warned us we were nuts not to invest in the real estate market. Nuts we manifestly were. But at least we were consistent. For the next fifty years, we never owned a house.

NORMAN SHERRY DROPPED a note in my English Department mailbox, proposing lunch. To introduce him to the local zeitgeist, I treated him to a burger and fries at the Nighthawk, "a Texas tradition since 1933." As I teased Sherry, this made it as ancient in local terms as Stonehenge.

Afterward I wrote to Greene that his biographer "seemed an earnest, pleasant and hardworking guy." This was the best I could manage. Greene didn't need me to remind him that Sherry was short and plump and had henna-dyed hair and a mustache that was all wrong for a scholar who so obviously tried to project an image of seriousness. Sherry asked me very few questions. The one I remember best was whether I believed Greene loved Yvonne Cloetta. I replied that I'd just be guessing. He encouraged me to go ahead and guess.

"Isn't that a question you'd be better off putting to Greene?" I said.

"It's hardly a thing one can ask a man about his mistress."

"Agreed. It's certainly not something I'd ask."

Sherry nodded and jotted in his Moleskine notebook, which he held close to the vest. This gesture, like his dyed hair and mustache, lent him the slightly louche appearance of a riverboat gambler.

In November, under pressure from the HRC, I once again broached with Greene the matter of a visit:

> Mr. [Warren] Roberts and the other members of the Humanities Research Center have still not given up hope that you'll come to Texas in April of 1977. Mr. Roberts and others have urged me to do whatever I could to persuade you. I think you know how much Linda and I would like to see you and have the opportunity to reciprocate some of the hospitality you've shown us . . . I've advised Mr. Rob-

erts-you might want to bring Yvonne—your secretary, I
explained to him—and he was in agreement. The main
thing I must stress is how eager everyone at Texas is to have
you visit. It is a particular source of pride to the University
to have your papers here, and they would like to have you
come and see how well they've taken care of them . . . If
there is anything about the travel arrangements or honorarium which might be improved and would change your
mind, please let us know.

Janet Malcolm, writing in the *New Yorker*, called letters
"fossils of feeling." Fifty years after the fact, it's difficult to guess
whether my correspondence with Greene always reflected my
feelings. Was I ever really that reverential and eager to please?
Did I overstep my authority and misrepresent the HRC's interest in Greene? No, that's not possible. The HRC not only read
my letters to Greene; they bought them for their collection.
The institution was and is omnivorous in its appetite.

Six weeks passed before Greene answered, in early 1977:

I have only just received on Dec. 31 your letter of November
27 because I have been away in Panama having a most interesting time with the General there. I am afraid I had to
refuse the invitation of Mr. Roberts and Dr. Glade because
I am in the last stages of a novel and I also have the idea
of a possible new novel set in Panama which will mean
returning there next July and I simply can't afford the time
for distractions. I feel I have wasted a lot of your time in
arranging things but perhaps when I am 80 I shall feel at
liberty to accept invitations.

Notorious for my short fuse and my less than forgiving nature, I nevertheless swallowed this frustration without protest. Instead, I redoubled my efforts to get my profile of Greene into print. When my agent failed to place it on the commercial market, I submitted it to literary magazines. I even tried to interest the *Texas Monthly* when it still looked likely that Greene would visit Austin. Rejection followed rejection.

A new start-up magazine, *Quest*, had invited me to contribute articles. It specialized in features about human courage and endurance, the pursuit of excellence, and the triumph over adversity. Interpreting its theme broadly, *Quest* had me review travel books by Peter Matthiessen and Ted Hoagland and a debunking biography about André Malraux. When I heard that Robert Penn Warren's wife, Eleanor Clark, herself a respected author, had been stricken with an eye ailment that was blinding her as she struggled to complete a final book, I suggested that I review *Eyes, Etc.: A Memoir*.

In the spirit of transparency, I advised *Quest* that I had met both Warren and Clark through my editor, Albert Erskine. Erskine had cautioned me that Eleanor was accustomed to getting what she wanted. When Albert Camus had visited New York City after WWII, she had courted him with a bouquet of flowers. Erskine urged me to "keep in mind that she doesn't mean to be as insulting as she sometimes sounds."

Quest trusted that I could be objective, and gave me the assignment, not altogether aware of how sympathetic I was toward Eleanor. One summer, while Warren was in Connecticut for medical treatment and their kids were off on a European bicycle tour, she had spent a few days with us at Montclair, swimming, hiking in the hills around Auribeau, and reading in the shade of pink oleanders. Every afternoon, she challenged me to a tennis match and made it clear she had no interest in hit-and-giggle games. She wanted to win. My enduring image of Eleanor Clark is of her at the opposite end of the tennis court, limned against the blue-green Alpes-Maritimes. For a woman of such elegance and refinement, she flung herself into every point with the same headlong abandon she deployed in literary debate. She wrote in *Eyes, Etc.* that she still took a stab at tennis, tracking the flight of the ball by sound as her sight failed. It broke my heart to read this, just as it did when she described how she worked with a Magic Marker on a yellow legal pad, scrawling a word or two per page in letters large enough to register on her deteriorating retinas.

As I was revising my review, Philip Mayer unexpectedly flew in from Dublin. He had recently been diagnosed with diabetes, and I assumed he had come to consult his doctor. Although conscientious about his diet and his insulin injections, he generally avoided discussing the disease. I could see that he had something on his mind. But I waited for him to tell me what was wrong.

To my shock, he said a rich, impatient Frenchman wanted to buy Montclair. Now that his children were grown, now that taxes on *maisons secondaires* had risen, now that Claire felt ill at ease whenever he was away and she was alone in the huge house . . . well, Philip hated to spring this on us without warning. He conceded that his health was also a factor in deciding to sell Montclair.

The prospective buyer insisted on closing the deal and moving in before the end of the summer. Philip stressed that he had delayed the contract to give us another month at Montclair—and to make a proposal. Was there any chance we'd like to buy Montclair if he lowered the price to rock bottom? He offered to let us have it for two hundred and fifty thousand dollars. The land alone was worth more than that. He was sorry he couldn't afford to let us have the place for free. But he planned to buy an apartment in Cannes and he needed cash for a down payment.

Touched by the gesture and shattered by the news, yet struggling not to show it, I said I couldn't imagine ever accumulating a quarter of a million dollars. My annual salary at UT was fifteen thousand dollars. My last book advance had been seventy-five hundred. I thanked Philip profusely for his hospitality over the years. He hadn't just allowed us to live privileged lives. The greatest privilege was his friendship. I knew I'd never meet another man as generous and kind.

Philip teared up. I feared I might cry. In those days, men didn't embrace and exchange cheek kisses. At least American men didn't. Philip settled for touching a hand to my shoulder and saying that as soon as he bought a new place, he hoped we'd visit him there.

Late in the season, we had difficulty renting another house, and we wound up in a converted garage near the perfume factories in Grasse. There was no pool, no tennis court, no lush garden, just swarms of mosquitoes that must have been attracted by the flowery scent of the factories. I finished off *Eyes, Etc.* and mailed the review to the literary editor at *Quest*, William Plummer. A poet himself, he counted Robert Penn Warren among his friends and let him read the review "as a courtesy." Plummer believed both Warren and Eleanor Clark would be delighted by it. He was badly mistaken.

I never heard from Warren, but his wife hated the piece and excoriated me in a letter for writing such sentimental slop. She complained that I made her sound like "a sob sister." Why had I focused on sympathy rather than the book's aesthetic merits? Other readers—she cited no names—had compared her prose to George Orwell's. That was the appropriate standard for evaluating her style—Orwell and his equals. As for my conclusion, paraphrasing Dylan Thomas about raging against the dying of the light, that was flat-out wrong. Shapes and colors were fading, not light.

Fortunately, Eleanor wrote, I had a chance to correct my factual and interpretive errors. *Quest* magazine had a three-month lead time, more than adequate for me to make the changes she demanded. In the long run, she said, *Quest* and I would profit from her criticism.

In the past, I had received the odd grumpy letter from an aggrieved author. But in fifty years of book reviewing, Eleanor Clark remains the only one who objected in advance to a positive review and insisted that it be recast in more favorable terms before publication.

William Plummer apologized and admitted that he should never have sent the review to Robert Penn Warren. He assured me he was satisfied with what I had submitted and intended to publish it unchanged.

I considered not replying to Eleanor. But it occurred to me that she might be more offended if I didn't acknowledge her objections. In an aerogram I wrote that I respected her POV and hoped she understood that *Quest* was a specialized publication, not a literary journal. George Orwell's lofty standards would be of less interest to its audience than the human virtues her memoir so nobly embodied.

Her scathing reply left her previous letter sounding like a gentle maternal remonstrance. She instructed me to read carefully what she wrote and "don't get your Irish up." First off, she decried my penmanship. Tiny and untidy, it had almost cost her the little eyesight she had left. Hereafter, she said, I should type.

Second, she demanded to know why I would ever lower myself to work for a magazine where style and intelligence weren't valued. I should challenge *Quest*'s editorial staff and its subscribers to raise their standards. If Orwell wasn't familiar to them, I needed to educate them. If they declined to learn, I should seek a better venue. It did no good, she said, to write down to readers. That would just ruin my prose, which already had weaknesses we could discuss later.

Even if my review was acceptable to *Quest*, Eleanor went on, that didn't make it worthwhile. She recalled that early in her career she had been headstrong and resistant to editorial advice. Once when she reviewed Katherine Anne Porter from a Marxist perspective, nattering on about politics instead of analyzing Porter's art, Philip Rahv, the editor of the *Partisan Review*, had persuaded her to rewrite the piece, and Eleanor was grateful that he had. Only a child or a fool, she concluded, wouldn't admit he was wrong and correct his errors.

With enormous effort I managed to control my egregious Irishness and calmly broadened the debate, as if we were a couple of panelists at the Ninety-second Street Y, shooting the breeze about the delicate balance between authors and reviewers. Of the thousands of books that appear each year, I wrote to Eleanor, the majority received no attention at all. Others fell into claws determined to draw blood. A happy few had the good fortune to get favorable treatment. The present system amounted to no more than a lottery. It needed to be improved. But was allowing literary royalty to read their reviews in advance and demand revisions really the answer? How would

Eleanor have reacted if Philip Rahv had shown her review to Katherine Anne Porter and permitted Porter to rewrite it?

My questions went unanswered. I never heard from Eleanor Clark again, nor did I hear from Robert Penn Warren. As for their good friend Albert Erskine, the editor of my first four novels, he said nothing about the incident and I never saw him again.

IX

◇◇◇◇◇◇◇

WHEN CONFRONTED BY his early work, Graham Greene observed that "the self of forty years ago is not the self of today and I read my book as a stranger would." I understand the sentiment, but don't necessarily subscribe to it. For almost five decades, my profile of Greene, "The Staying Power and the Glory," has never been far from my mind. Originally written in 1975, it languished unpublished for two years until *The Nation* picked it up for seventy-five dollars in the United States and the *London Magazine* paid thirty pounds for the U.K. rights. Having lived with feelings of failure for so long, I experienced little satisfaction, just a sense of relief, when it finally came out. Down to this day the piece retains its power to rile me.

Before we relocated from the infested converted garage to Italy, in September 1977, I mailed the profile to Greene along with an apology that Alan Ross, editor of the *London Magazine*, had not sent a copy immediately, as I had asked him to. Perhaps the dust-up with Eleanor Clark accounts for the cringing apologetic tone of my letter to Greene. It certainly wasn't any awareness of the flaws in "The Staying Power and the Glory." Only later did I realize how many amateur mistakes I had committed—conflating conversations that occurred at different times into a seamless narrative, neglecting to double-check facts, and inserting quote marks around material that I might have been wiser to paraphrase. As a favor to Greene, I had omitted any mention of Yvonne, and I deleted unflattering details, such as Greene's acid disparagement of Jacques Cloetta and his sophomoric pranks, especially the one he played on Linda with the hemorrhoid applicator.

"I hope you like it," I wrote to Greene. "Or if you dislike it, I hope you'll understand how my urge to write and publish it sprang from my deep respect for you."

THE STAYING POWER AND THE GLORY

NIGHTS ARE NO longer so tender in Antibes. Although the village hasn't taken on the tawdriness of Miami Beach or the tackiness of southern Spain, it has, like every resort along the Côte d'Azur, changed drastically in the decades since Scott and Zelda were here amusing themselves and horrifying the French by smashing crystal, wrecking cars, and falling down stairs. Perhaps it is simply that these days the rich aren't so different from you and me. In summer it seems half of Europe has descended on the Riviera, and tourists rattle into town on motorbikes and Renaults rather than in Rolls-Royces, and they stay in condominiums and threadbare *pensions* instead of at the Hôtel du Cap or private villas. Their rubber rafts and runabouts bob brazenly in the paths of mighty yachts, and their bodies, bared to the legal limit and basted with Bain de Soleil, have the impudence to turn as bronze as any jet setter's.

That evening as I left the Grande Corniche and headed for the coast, traffic advanced through the walls of Antibes like an army of ants. The maze of streets in the Old City was clotted with cars, choked with exhaust fumes, and as I circled past the port searching for a parking place, I noticed hot dog stands, snack bars, and everybody, regardless of age or shape, dressed in blue denim.

On a quieter street occupied almost entirely by a modern apartment building, I found the address and pressed a buzzer. The door opened electronically, and from a bare, antiseptic lobby, the kind that gives a look of impermanence and impersonality to air terminals, I went up to meet the man who is often called the greatest living novelist in the English language.

Graham Greene is tall, well over six feet, and looks much younger than seventy-three. If he does stoop slightly at the shoulders, it is not as if bowed by years but as though to incline his ear and listen closer. Only his eyes betray his age. Moist, large, and often fixed on something in the distance, they also seem sad. But then they have seen a lot. I apologized for being late, and blamed the traffic I had run into returning from an exhibition of Nicholas de Staël's painting in St. Paul de Vence.

"There's where he killed himself, you know." Greene waved through his living room, out the double doors, to a narrow balcony. But he was gesturing, I thought, toward Ft. Vauban. "He jumped off the wall. It doesn't look high enough, but it worked." He led me onto the terrace to have a look. Though we stood four or five floors above the street, the noise was nearly deafening, and we had to raise our voices.

"The traffic goes on until all hours," Greene lamented, "and everyone in the building has a barbecue on his balcony. They keep me up half the night chattering over their dinners. Some mornings I'm almost too tired to work."

What time did he start working? How long did he stay at it? I asked, sounding like the rawest amateur hoping to discover some secret in the details of his schedule.

"I'm usually awake by six and keep going until I have a hundred words. That means about five hours. I have to be strict with myself or I'd never get anything done. I used to write five hundred words a day, but as I got older, I found that was too much. So I cut down to three hundred, then to one hundred, just to keep my hand in." When he smiled, his eyelids creased and the moistness of his pupils seemed about to spill out. "I never lose track of where I am. Sometimes I stop smack in the middle of a paragraph."

Difficult as this was to believe, Greene swore it was true. "Of course I used to work much faster. Back when I was young, I liked to bring out a new book every year. It was a conscious reaction against the Bloomsbury people, most of whom seemed content to do a few things, build a huge reputation, and rest on it. But even then I always had to revise my novels again and again to get them right. Now it takes me years to finish a book, and sometimes it still isn't right."

I remarked how strange it was that practice and experience didn't make life much easier for a novelist. "You'd think once a writer had been through it a few times and developed confidence in his talent . . ."

"One has no talent," Greene interrupted. "I have no talent. It's just a question of working, of being willing to put in the time."

As WE STARED off silently at the wall where de Staël had killed himself, I thought about how Greene's modesty, his insistence on privacy, and his refusal to accept more than the most grudging credit for his accomplishments set him apart from so many writers of this century. He is roughly a contemporary of the flamboyant American authors Fitzgerald and Hemingway, who are always associated with the South of France and with Gerald Murphy's enclave at Antibes. (The same generation produced Faulkner, Wolfe, and Steinbeck.) In those days, Hemingway had taken as his motto the French aphorism *"Il faut d'abord durer."* To accomplish anything, one first had to last. And yet it is Greene, a discreet, self-effacing Englishman, who has lasted and continued to write—five hours, every day, one hundred words—while others burned themselves out, died young, committed suicide, slipped into obscurity, or let themselves ossify into literary landmarks.

In 1973, when his most recent novel, *The Honorary Consul*, was published, it received worldwide acclaim and quickly became a best seller. But apart from the commercial and critical success, it was far more remarkable that a sixty-nine-year-old novelist was still performing at the height of his powers, still writing from firsthand experience about the Third World and revolution, still pursuing ultimate questions about life, death, and belief. In a sense, *The Honorary Consul* can be seen as a companion piece to *The Power and the Glory*, a gauge of the political and philosophical distance the world has traveled in the last four decades. Whereas the priest in *The Power and the Glory* overcomes his cowardice and preserves his faith despite the religious persecution of a left-wing military dictatorship, the priest in *The Honorary Consul* becomes a revolutionary and abandons the Church, which has allied itself with a right-wing military dictatorship.

The turnabout surprised some readers. "It shouldn't have," said Greene, whose sympathy has always been with individuals, not dogma. "The book doesn't contradict what I wrote earlier. It only expresses my feelings better. It's rather a relief not to have to be told that my best work lies thirty or forty years in the past. Every time I pick up a newspaper and read about another political kidnapping, I think *The Honorary Consul* may have been a few years ahead of the times."

Greene has long had this sense of timeliness, an instinct for stories that afterward seem prophetic and a tropism for troubled corners of the world. In Africa, in Saigon and Hanoi, in Malaysia, in Haiti, in Central and South America, he has produced not only dozens of novels, short stories, and travel books, but controversial articles on the Mau Mau uprising in Kenya, influential reviews of hundreds of movies and books, and interviews with Ho Chi Minh, Diem, and Castro, a record which even Oriana Fallaci would envy.

Age hasn't stopped Greene, nor have success and celebrity compromised his integrity. He won't hustle his books and he refuses to withdraw to the comfortable embrace of any of the universities which have offered him sinecures.

FROM GREENE'S NOVELS, most readers know something of his experiences in revolutionary Mexico in the

1930s, wartime West Africa in the 1940s, more wars and insurrections in East Africa, Malaysia, Cuba, and Indochina in the 1950s. But throughout the 1960s and on into the 1970s—Greene's sixties and seventies as well as this century's—he has continued to travel, to grow with the times rather than rail at them, and to put himself on the spot.

In 1967 he was in the Sinai, pinned down by artillery fire across the Suez Canal. In August 1968, he hurried to Prague to support Dubĉek and protest the Russian invasion. While other writers grumbled and wondered about general conditions in South America and the specific situation in Allende's Chile, Greene made it a point to go there every year, monitored as usual by the CIA. ("We're waiting for you," an American voice warned him by telephone his first night in Santiago.) Then in autumn of 1973, when *The Honorary Consul* was about to appear in America, he refused to do a promotional tour and instead flew to South Africa, where it had been arranged for him to hold secret meetings with various rebel groups.

It would be difficult to think of any author who has written more often and more effectively about the bankruptcy of colonial and postcolonial regimes, the abuses of political power, the threat of unrestrained intelligence agencies, and the repression of personal and religious beliefs, whether by the left or the right. In a world that likes to pay lip service to writers who are fiercely independent and politically *engagé*, and who risk great danger to do their jobs, no one except Solzhenitsyn—certainly not Hemingway, Camus, Malraux, or Sartre—can make the kinds of claims which, interestingly enough, Graham Greene declines to make for himself.

As the lights in Antibes began to blink on, we went inside. The living room walls were lined with books, but there was very little to suggest who lived there. Perhaps the personal memorabilia are in Greene's apartment in Paris or his house on Capri. Or then again, maybe he prefers to keep his personal life tucked away, his day-to-day existence unencumbered by the past.

While Greene mixed us each a Scotch and Perrier ("You Americans like ice, don't you?" This American did), I told him I had always enjoyed his books, but admired even more his energy, courage, and commitment. He dismissed the compliment, saying straight out that he was a coward. He was frequently afraid and suffered from a long list of phobias: "I'm terrified of water, for example. Always have been. It's all I can do to splash my face in the morning and rinse away the shaving cream."

As he proceeded to tell of spending months in Tahiti, scuba diving every day in a vain attempt to conquer his fear, I pointed out what appeared obvious. It was a triumph of bravery to spend hours in the ocean if you were pathologically afraid of water. Greene shook his head. He was still a coward, he said, even though he'd forced himself to go diving. In a way it was a replay of his attitude toward his talent. Inverting the biblical homily, Greene in effect claimed you couldn't judge him by his works but only by the weaknesses he felt within. Perhaps this paradigm of his reasoning explained the paradoxical nature of his fictional characters, who have to be strong because they know they are weak, who are good because they are sinners.

After the discussion of cowardice, there came an uncomfortable moment and we quietly sipped our drinks. Greene has a reputation of resisting interviews, being uncooperative in conversation and chary of personal disclosures. It may simply be that people hold unrealistic expectations of writers and assume that anyone whose medium is language is perfectly at ease in conversation. But the connection between the spoken and the written word is tenuous at best, and many novelists, loquacious though they may be by nature, have learned the hard way to avoid idle conversation with journalists.

"It's gotten so I hate to say who I am or what I believe," Greene admitted. "A few years ago I told an interviewer I'm a Gnostic. The next day's newspaper announced that I had become an agnostic."

For Greene, anecdote appears to provide a more comfortable vehicle for exploring past experience and a most effective means of communicating with strangers. Certainly he is seldom as animated or interesting as when he is telling a story. When, to break the silence, I said I liked the painting on the wall behind his couch, he explained it had been a gift from Fidel Castro and suddenly we were launched for several hours.

Greene had visited Cuba while Castro and his men were fighting in the mountains, and through intermediaries, he managed to contact the rebels and arrange a meeting. When the interview went well, he asked if there wasn't some way he could return the favor, and Castro had said yes. Come back and talk again and bring warm clothing. It was cold in the mountains, especially at night, and his men were freezing.

Since Greene suspected he was being watched by Batista's police, he didn't see how he could smuggle supplies over the circuitous route to their rendezvous point. There was also the danger of compromising his journalist's neutrality.

But Castro convinced him he didn't need a truck-load of contraband, just sweaters, pairs of socks, and trousers. Greene could claim he was cold. Weren't the English always cold, even in the tropics?

So Greene bundled up like an Eskimo, suffered through the sweltering heat of the lowlands, reached the mountains and molted a few layers of clothing, then returned to Havana pounds lighter.

Years afterward, when Castro was in power, Greene came back to Cuba, presumably more appropriately dressed for the occasion. It was then that Castro presented him the painting in gratitude for his help during the revolution.

I asked if Cuba had changed much, and he said, "Oh yes, for the average Cuban it's a far better place. But . . . well, it's too bad about Havana. It used to be such a lively city. Now it seems sort of dreary."

Then abruptly we were discussing Haiti. Perhaps there was a transition. If so, I was unaware of it. Yet I had no sense that Greene was taking tangents. For one thing, as an accomplished raconteur, he had the ability to control a listener just as skillfully as he set up a reader. His hands, in particular, he used to good effect, clasping them in his lap, then letting them fly out at dramatic moments. For another thing, there was a kind of cartographical logic to his vignettes and he connected distantly spaced dots on the map and circled the globe as unerringly as a latitudinal line.

I myself had once been in Port-au-Prince during what was described as an abortive coup. Electricity was cut throughout the city, tourists were hustled into their hotels, and ill-tempered troops patrolled the streets. Only later was it revealed that Papa Doc Duvalier, trapped in the bathroom during the course of a family squabble, had pressed an emergency button to signal his guards to rescue him from the john. As a comic Caribbean dictator, Duvalier might have been invented by Greene's friend Evelyn Waugh—if, that is, Papa Doc hadn't been deadly as well as ridiculous.

"Did you know I put him in the publishing business?" asked Greene. "After *The Comedians* came out, Duvalier went into a rage and threatened to get revenge. But rather than order one of his voodoo priests to put a hex on me, he had somebody write up a crazy attack on me. A whole book of nonsense privately printed at Papa Doc's expense. I'm really rather proud of it. I went to a lot of trouble to get a copy and I wouldn't part with it for anything." He found the book and passed it to me. A collage of photographs, forged documents, and lunacy, it sought to portray Haiti as a tranquil and progressive paradise and Graham Greene as inaccurate, dishonest, and an infamous racist.

"I wish Papa Doc had come over to the British West Indies. I would have introduced him to what may be a branch of my family, descendants of my ancestors who owned plantations there. They're Black. One little boy has my name."

We moved, not unnaturally it seemed, to a discussion of movies. He still likes films but no longer sees as many as he did when he was a critic for the *Spectator*, and he doesn't much care to be around movie people. It's been years since he's taken the short drive up the coast to Cannes for the film festival. And yet, not long ago, he made a surreptitious screen debut.

Near Antibes, François Truffaut shot *Day for Night*, a movie whose subject was essentially the difficulties of making a movie. As the original title suggested—*La Nuit américaine* is the technique for filming night scenes during the day—Truffaut meant to show how cinematic verisimilitude depends on mechanical devices, how actors, for all their foibles, can produce art, and how illusion can lead to truth.

When one of the actors in the movie within the movie is killed, an insurance agent flies down from London to determine whether a claim should be paid and the film should proceed or be canned. The insurance agent has a bit part, but a pivotal one, and Truffaut, dissatisfied with all the professional actors available, put out a public call for an Englishman of a certain age. Graham Greene saw the advertisement and auditioned for the role under an assumed name. Truffaut was favorably impressed; this Englishman seemed authentic, just the sort to play a seedy, calculating insurance agent.

Only later, as Truffaut was watching the rushes, did someone in the screening room moan, "My God, that's Graham Greene." At first Truffaut was angry and upset that during his lighthearted exploration of the relationship between illusion and reality he had been duped, a victim of his own illusions; then he was embarrassed that he hadn't recognized Greene, a writer whose work he admired. Truffaut telephoned, apologized profusely, and promised to cut the scene. But Greene said there was no need for apologies, he had enjoyed himself and wanted to be in the movie. In that case, Truffaut assured him, he could count on seeing his name in the credits.

No, Greene didn't want that either and made Truffaut swear he wouldn't mention his name. "I was curious to see if anyone would notice," Greene explained. "Very few did, and I was delighted by the secret."

Although *Day for Night* was released in the United States virtually at the same time *The Honorary Consul* was published, he never exploited the incident. Content to enjoy his secret, he called no press conferences, provided no self-serving leaks to news agencies. One can only surmise how another novelist might have acted under the same circumstances.

IT WAS INEVITABLE, I suppose, that I would eventually try to work the conversation around to Vietnam. Greene knew the country and conflict as few people did, having gone there before Dien Bien Phu and defined the tragedy taking shape for America long before the Marines arrived, before Tet and the truce and the spring of 1975's sudden unraveling. But at this subject, his volubility faltered. He could do an imitation of Diem's hysterically high-pitched laugh, and he told a final, self-deprecating tale, this one about his meeting with Ho Chi Minh, which had made him so nervous beforehand that he smoked a pipe of opium.

But as for the war itself, and America's military policy, he had little to say. What was there to say that he hadn't said before? In the opinion of most experts, *The Quiet American* is still the best novel about the war, and when one considers that it was published more than twenty years ago, it seems all the more appallingly prophetic. So

Greene would only repeat that he loved the Vietnamese and especially the city of Saigon, which in those days had a laundered look each morning and smelled flowery and full of life. When asked if he'd like to go back, he said he preferred to remember it as it had been.

The scent of charcoal smoke had insinuated itself into the room. Out on the balconies everybody was barbecuing. It promised to be a long, restless night and a difficult morning for Greene. As I got up to leave, I asked what he was working on now. I had waited until the end so he would feel free to duck the question. But he said he had recently picked up a novel which he had set aside years ago. Although he was making progress, he wasn't sure he would finish it or how it would turn out if he did. "I put the book away when that Kim Philby business blew up. I was well into it by then but there are certain similarities between my plot and the Philby affair, and I didn't want anyone to think I had drawn on that. There has already been enough nonsense about my friendship with Philby. Perhaps now the novel can be read on its own terms."

As WE HEADED for the door, he added that he was also collecting some of his autobiographical sketches. A sequel to *A Sort of Life*? I asked. Not exactly. Just isolated pieces and a few articles that still seemed worthwhile to him.

In the hall now, I said if the anecdotes he had told me were in the collection, it was bound to be a fascinating book.

"I don't know," he said. "Interesting experiences, fascinating people you meet in extraordinary places—

of course that's all very enjoyable. But they don't make one a better writer and they don't always make for good books." As we descended in the elevator, Greene went on, "I sometimes think failure and boredom, the feeling of loneliness, of being flat and empty, have more influence on a novelist."

When we reached the lobby we shook hands, and then I was out on the street, wondering about the final paradox Greene had presented. In the elevator he seemed to have been suggesting that although he wrote successful and compelling novels, it was out of a sense of failure and boredom; although he had led an exciting life, it was just an effort to overcome a feeling of hollowness and drift.

But it seemed to me Greene had indulged in self-deprecation one time too often. If anything had become clear that evening, it was that Graham Greene is a good man because he has always had a moral compass, a courageous man because he is willing to go where the compass points, and a gifted writer because he has the ability to make the reader understand and follow the compass too.

The town of Antibes may have changed since Fitzgerald, and all those who came after him, prowled this coast searching for some vision of grace and dignity that would endure after innocence ends. But Graham Greene has lasted and will last.

X

WEEKS, AS THEY tend to do in Rome at the smoky end of summer, dissolved into a dry white wine sky. Then one of the familiar blue envelopes with no return address arrived. It was thicker than normal, and because bad news usually arrives as thin and desiccated as a corpse, I expected good news. But Greene's reaction to "The Staying Power and the Glory" hit me like . . . simile serves no purpose. To appreciate the impact of his letter, one has to read it.

Antibes
14th September 1977

Dear Mike,

I only saw a copy of your article in *London Magazine* just as I was leaving for Panama and so I can only express my real horror at it now on my return. I don't think that any journalist has done worse for me than you who are such a promising novelist. I very much resented the inaccuracies and the bits of dialogue which I had never spoken put between inverted commas. At least a journalist doesn't attribute his mistakes to his victim. I have annotated every page of the *London Magazine* and I propose to sell it for a large sum if I can. The first inaccuracy, in the first line, describing Antibes as a village when it has 50,000 inhabitants was amusing but what followed was not amusing. I never told you that de Staël jumped off the Fort Carré—he jumped off the ramparts. I have never taken five hours to write a hundred words. I very much doubt if I said that I had no talent. It doesn't sound like me at all. Considering the other things you put in my mouth I think this is another of your novelist's inventions. I never said that I thought that *The Honorary Consul* might have been a few years ahead of the times as my best news story is that I found a similar kidnapping happened in Argentina when I was there and I thought I would have to abandon the book. I have never been offered a sinecure at any university. I was not warned my first night in Santiago by the CIA. No one has ever been stupid enough to propose that I should do a promotional tour. I probably said that I was afraid of drowning but [. . .] I have never scuba dived in my life. I probably told you that I did practise with a mask which is a very different thing in Tahiti. All your account of Cuba is completely false. I have only met Castro once long after the revolution. The idea that I would wear double layers of clothing in Santiago in a hot December is absurd. You could have found an accurate account of the affair in the Introduction to the Collected Edition of *Our Man in Havana*. There is not a word of truth in what you have given of the Cuban affair. No little boy in St. Kitt's has my name. One little girl may be a cousin. Your whole account of the affair with Truffaut is untrue and not as I gave it to you. How unutterably silly it is to suggest that I should have called a press conference about the affair. I never went to my meeting with Ho Chi Minh "stoned." I had merely had a couple of pipes of opium in the old town and as my ration was normally ten pipes I was certainly not stoned. You write that I have the ability to make the reader understand and follow the compass, but it must be a pretty dangerous compass if the one manufactured by you.

I am sorry to be angry about this article but it gave me a great deal of pain for its inaccuracies and its absurdities especially when the absurdities were put into inverted commas. I can see that a novelist is far worse than a journalist. I don't think any journalist has made so many mistakes in so few pages. I am sending a copy of this letter to Norman Sherry because I do not want any would-be biographer to be misled by all these inaccuracies. I think we had better not speak of this deplorable article ever again.

Yours,
[Signed] Graham

Days passed before I composed myself sufficiently to compose a response to Greene. His anger would have gutted me under any circumstances, but it was all the more wounding after what I had gone through with Eleanor Clark. Attacked by another author I had praised, I floundered, trying to decide whether to defend myself or simply apologize and disappear down a dark hole. Greene's threat to annotate the article and sell it to the highest bidder, and his vow to copy his letter to Norman Sherry, raised the prospect of his humiliating accusations being published in English newspapers, then being repeated in his authorized biography.

For fear that Alan Ross would be blindsided, I alerted the editor of *London Magazine* to Greene's complaints. Ross had long been a prominent figure in the English literary firmament. An author of memoirs, poetry, travel books, and cricket coverage for the *Guardian*, he operated *London Magazine* out of his hip pocket. His reaction to Greene's fury was one of drawling equanimity. He observed that Greene was, after all, a fiction writer and a spy whose nonfiction sometimes stretched the truth. Ross speculated that Greene, under the influence of alcohol, had embroidered the anecdotes he recounted to me, then once they were in print, he felt obliged to deny having said anything of the sort. It was part of a pattern, Ross pointed out, this contrast between the iron discipline of Greene's professional life and the disarray of his personal life.

Still, I felt betrayed, and who knew better than Greene the pain of betrayal. My belligerent instinct was to fight back. Out of self-respect, if nothing else, I believed Greene deserved a blunt response. I had, after all, offered to show him the profile in advance. If I had made journalistic mistakes, I had also taken steps to protect his reputation and privacy by deleting details that an experienced, hardnosed reporter would have seized on.

Rome
October 6, 1977

Dear Graham,

Needless to say, I am sorry you reacted as you did, and although I can understand how you wouldn't want to hear any more about it, I don't believe you can honestly expect me to remain silent.

Your horror, resentment and anger at my article could not have been greater than my astonishment, disillusionment, and yes, anger, at your letter. Repeatedly you accuse me of inaccuracies, falsehoods, misrepresentations of fact and erroneous quotations. You don't come out and call me a liar, but the word hovers over almost every sentence, even when—perhaps in politeness, perhaps in sarcasm—you attribute everything to my novelist's inventiveness.

It seems not to have occurred to you that when we talked there were two novelists in the room. I should have kept that fact foremost in my mind and not been so gullible. It also seems not to have occurred to you that we were not alone. Linda was with us. Her memory on most details in the article, especially of the anecdotes you told, is the same as mine. My notebooks, many of my letters, some of your letters to me, and various article proposals that I began making in February of 1973—all of them safely preserved at the University of Texas [at the HRC] along with your own papers—will provide additional corroboration of what I wrote. Of course you can always claim Linda is lying and I falsified my notes and that I invented everything. But what imaginable motive would we have? Why would I write an article which was entirely favorable about you, continue for two years in my efforts to get it published, and finally sell it to *London Magazine* for the grand sum of £30 if I knew it was full of falsehoods? If the information and, more specifically, the anecdotes, didn't come from you, where did they come from? Quite frankly, some of them are so good, if I had invented them, I would have used them in my own fiction—which is perhaps what you should have done with them.

It is interesting that after accusing me of misquoting you, you proceed to misread and misinterpret much of what I wrote. It is almost as if you hoped to catch me on one or two small factual errors so that you could claim everything was wrong. If one thing was mistaken, then everything had to be. I don't know how else to explain your niggling and your refusal to comprehend what is on the page.

To start where you did—I referred to Antibes as a village only in the sense that it had changed and was therefore no longer a village, no longer the sort of place Fitzgerald and Hemingway had frequented. Every sentence in the first two paragraphs conveys an impression of Antibes' size, congestion, etc.

As for the ramparts de Staël jumped from, do you mean the ramparts of the town or of the fort? It's unclear from your letter. It was also unclear that evening when you pointed out your window and said precisely the words on the page. I'm sorry to have made it seem you didn't know where de Staël killed himself. The mistake is mine, but the words are yours.

As for your work schedule, I questioned you closely and you said you worked five hours a day and usually did a hundred words. Now perhaps you do a hundred words in a certain time and then use the rest of the five hours to review what you've written. And perhaps things have changed since we spoke about that. [In a letter in 1972, Greene lamented that he was reduced to writing two hundred words a day.] At that time, July 1972, you said you thought *The Honorary Consul* would be your last novel.

You seemed to have very little hope of finishing the new novel [*The Human Factor*] that comes out this winter. You mentioned that you were doing a hundred words a day just to keep your hand in. I was particularly struck by this and much admired your meticulousness and staying power.

Doubt all you like, but you did say "One has no talent. I have no talent." It's not the sort of quote one forgets when one is a young unknown novelist talking to an older, renowned writer. And frankly, it does sound like you. Although of course you have a sense of yourself and of your great worth as a novelist you do tend to shrug off compliments and to speak on occasion self-deprecatingly. What you said certainly didn't tempt me to agree that you have no talent.

As for *The Honorary Consul* being ahead of the times, I believe you have been much too literal-minded and have misread the passage. It was clear from the context of our conversation—and clear, I think, to any reader—that you weren't claiming *The Honorary Consul* dealt with an unprecedented event. You were pointing out, in response to my comment about the book's timeliness, that the great spate of political kidnappings didn't come to dominate the daily news until the early '70s, but that you had been writing about these topics much earlier.

You're right, nobody is offered a sinecure. He's offered a job, or in the case of the university, a position or lectureship, which turns out to be a sinecure. When I asked whether you had had offers from universities, you said you had turned them all down. At our house at lunch, I listened as a professor offered you a position. You passed it off so quickly, perhaps you've forgotten. If sinecure is the word that offends you, I'm sorry. I should have said you had had offers and refused them. But the point remains the same. I was praising you for not turning into an academic circuit rider, as have so many American and British authors.

"I was not warned my first night in Santiago by the CIA." This claim comes as such a stunning denial of an anecdote which you told at least twice in my presence, I don't really know what to say. Is it possible you were warned not the first night, but some other night? Not in Santiago, but in some other city? Or are you disavowing the entire incident? The reason I remember the story so well is that it didn't make much sense. In fact I asked you whether there wasn't a chance it had been a misunderstanding. A wrong number? Why would the CIA tip its hand? You interpreted the call as simple intimidation.

In June 1973 I asked whether you'd be coming to America for the publication of *The Honorary Consul*. You said Michael Korda at Simon and Schuster wanted you to help promote the book, but you had no intention of doing so. You then told an amusing anecdote about being on an awful book chat show in London, and said you'd never do it again.

After I complimented you on your courage, you brought up your fear of water—something you also deal with in *A Sort of Life*. I know the difference between scuba diving and using a snorkel and mask. But the word *scuba*, which has a specific meaning, is misused all the time, and that may account for why I misheard what you said. It's possible you said you practiced with a scuba mask and I took that to mean you wore air tanks and dived. Sorry for the mistake. But does it change my point? A man who is afraid of drowning, yet makes himself go into the water, is no coward.

Concerning the Cuban anecdote I am altogether baffled. I have reported exactly what you told me. It is ludicrous to assume that I made it up. Even if you're not willing to give me any credit for decency, honesty, or morality, I hope you'll grant that I'm not dumb enough to have concocted such a story. Since I was trying to enhance your reputation, why would I tell such an extravagant lie and thereby injure your reputation? How on earth could I have thought I'd get away with it? After all, I sent you a copy of the article.

You write, "The idea that I would wear double layers of clothing in Santiago in hot December is absurd." Who said anything about Santiago? Not I. And my article contains no mention of "in hot December." I remember precisely what you told me and nothing you say in the introduction to *Our Man in Havana* will make me forget that.

The same applies to your story about St. Kitts. Is it possible that your own narrative genius got the best of you? That you indulged in a little tall tale telling, never thinking I'd repeat the story in print? How would I even have thought to have given you a branch of black relatives? And why?

Ditto the affair with Truffaut. Perhaps to put the best interpretation on this incident—and on many others—you don't remember what you told me.

I did not suggest you should have called a press conference. Far from it. I praised you for not doing anything of the sort, and I contrasted your behavior with other writers who would have milked the incident for every drop of publicity.

There doesn't seem to be any decent way of ending this letter. I can only repeat the same litany of questions—why would I have made up quotes and anecdotes you now claim are false? If I had made them up, why would I have sent you a copy of the article?

If you have annotated every page of *London Magazine* and mean to publish it as a way of undercutting my article or accusing me of gross distortion and inaccuracy, I'm afraid I'm not going to let that go unchallenged. Although I'm well aware my name doesn't carry the weight yours does, I do have a witness and I do have various documents which should corroborate what I wrote.

You and I may not speak "of this deplorable article ever again," but I believe a lot of other people will if you go ahead and press the issue. For your sake, I hope that you don't. Both Linda and I have a great deal of affection for you, and I hate to think of this unpleasantness dragging on to no purpose.

Yours,
[Signed] Mike

* * * * *

Antibes
28th October 1977

Dear Mike,

I am not accusing you of being a liar—I am accusing you of being a bad reporter who should use a tape-recorder, because your memory is far from being as trustworthy as you seem to believe. Perhaps I should not have dwelt on all the small errors like turning my little black cousin Claudette in St. Kitts into a small boy (I assure you that I am unlikely to make such a mistake) and the "ramparts" which only have one meaning to an Antibois into the Fort Vauban, and a simple mask into a scuba outfit which I would never have the courage to use. But such small errors, with which your Truffaut story too is packed, are only a matter for irritation and an indication of your untrustworthy memory.

The Cuban story is another affair. By defending it you suggest I am a liar—either to you, or to the public in the version of the story which is printed in my Introduction to *Our Man in Havana*. Your account also makes me into a rather boastful name dropper. I only met Castro once for some three hours in 1966 long after the revolution. It was not he but one of his agents in Havana who asked me to take a suitcase of sweaters and warm clothes to Santiago.

Why Santiago you ask? Perhaps you are confused by all the Santiagos in my life—in Cuba, in Chile, in Spain, in Panama. The answer is because the city was Batista's military H.Q. and there was an internal customs at the airport. I would have been able to explain away the warm clothes I was carrying in a suitcase as I was on my way to spend Christmas with my daughter in Canada. The idea that I wore them on top of my own clothes is quite incredible—the heat being somewhere in the nineties. Anyone with a knowledge of Cuba would put down the story you recount as a lie—a lie of mine, not a mistake of yours. The number of false stories in circulation about me through untrustworthy reporting is large, and I have every reason to point out untruths when they occur to Norman Sherry

who is working on a biography and working very hard in
the interests of accuracy. Of course I don't mind your sending him a copy of that rambling and rather offensive letter
of yours. He will be able to judge.

> Yours
> [Signed] Graham
> Professor Norman Sherry
> Alan Ross, Esq.

* * * * *

Rome
November 15, 1977

Dear Graham,

I'll start this letter just as I did my letter of October 6 by
saying I'm sorry. I'm sorry first that you found my letter
offensive. It was meant to explain, not offend.

Secondly, I'm sorry you thought it was rambling. It addressed itself point by point to the subjects raised by your
letter of September 14.

From personal experience and from seeing *Rashomon*, I
realize the futility of disputing matters and memories which
depend largely on point of view. I can only say that my account of the Cuban story was not intended to portray you as
a liar or as a name dropper, and I'm sorry if anyone gets that
mistaken impression—although I rather doubt anyone will.

At the risk of irritating you further, I would like to
point out an example of how small things—matters of
emphasis or intonation, elliptical statements or imprecise

antecedents—help promulgate the false stories which you decry. On Sept. 14 you wrote in your letter that on St. Kitts "One little girl *may* be a cousin." By Oct. 28 the subjunctive mood has disappeared and you write of "my little black cousin Claudette." If a disinterested party read only one of these sentences, he would likely draw a much different conclusion about whether you had black relatives on St. Kitts than if he had read the other. That is to say if he heard you speak about your "little black cousin Claudette," he would feel a lot more confident when he told someone else, "Graham Greene has a little black cousin." And yet, judging by your earlier letter, this might be wrong, since you leave the impression she may or may not be your cousin.

I'm not quibbling or splitting hairs here. I'm just saying that all of us make statements which lead to mistaken conclusions, especially when we assume the other person already knows what we're talking about. It seems to me that in the case of the Cuban story, you assumed I was familiar with the Introduction to *Our Man in Havana*—which I wasn't—and this may have led you to delete transitions and particulars which you thought I knew. If you'll read page 41 of the article, you'll notice I mention the jarring and disjointed nature of our conversation, i.e. that the logic of the vignettes was "cartographical." Thus while you supposed I knew you were talking about one of Castro's agents, I assumed you were referring to Castro himself, since the anecdote had been spurred by my comment about a picture which you explained he had given you.

You're right, a tape recorder would have eliminated the possibility of errors, but if you'll recall, I had *not* come to interview you that night or any other time. And it wasn't until years later that I decided to do an article based on those conversations—a fact which I apprised you of and to which you raised no objections.

Finally I'm sorry you think of me as a bad reporter. Actually, I'm not a reporter at all, but rather a novelist who was writing, not a piece of journalism, but rather a personal homage to you. I regret that it has caused you inconvenience, irritation, and pain. Perhaps my reasons for writing the article don't much matter to you, but they do to me and nothing of your reaction can diminish my respect for your work, my admiration for your courage and commitment, and my personal regard and gratitude to you.

> Yours,
> [Signed] Mike
> cc: Prof. Norman Sherry
> Alan Ross, Esq.

* * * * *

Antibes
30 November 1977

Dear Mike,

Let's forget all about it. I hope you are having a good time in Italy.

> A happy Christmas to you both.
> Yours ever,
> [Signed] Graham

XI

ⵧⵧⵧⵧⵧⵧ

To MY BAFFLEMENT, the storm seemed to have blown over as swiftly as it had boiled up. But I wasn't convinced that Greene had capitulated. I believed it possible he had decided it wasn't worth arguing about and had just kissed me off. On the other hand, he had often claimed "there's nothing like a fight to cure depression." Maybe excoriating me had been good medicine for a black mood, and the fact that I had fought back had set our friendship on a new footing instead of destroying it. Or so I attempted to persuade myself.

Because both Greene and I had copied our correspondence to Norman Sherry, I made it a point to discuss the imbroglio with the authorized biographer. He may have been telling me what he believed I wanted to hear, but he said Greene's letters to me had appalled him. According to Sherry, he had confronted Greene, asking what he could expect if Greene treated a friend so harshly.

Sherry let me read a line from Greene's journal that he intended to quote in Volume II. "If anybody tries to write a biography of me, how complicated they are going to find it and how misled they are going to be." Sherry explained that in Greene's determination to distort the record of his life, he sometimes went so far as to jot false entries in his diary, creating an alternate version of the historical record.

Months later, *Grazie*, an Italian magazine, asked permission to reprint the Greene profile. I advised them that Greene had vehemently objected to the accuracy of the article. Mondadori, the media empire that published Greene's books in Italy, also owned *Grazia*. The magazine's editors assured me that the profile would be submitted to Greene for approval. Perhaps Mondadori never followed through on contacting him. Maybe Greene asked for no changes. Whatever, when it appeared in translation, the profile repeated verbatim the original text.

Like a vampire that didn't die even after it was spiked in the heart with a wooden stake, the profile refused to stay buried. As I wrote Greene:

> I was startled recently to hear from *Playboy* magazine which, you may recall, originally assigned me to do that article on you. *Playboy* maintains that since they paid me an advance for the piece, they had an option to pick it up and publish it in their foreign editions. They say the Spanish edition of *Playboy* has expressed interest . . .
>
> I've told *Playboy* that under no circumstances should the article be published until/unless the inaccuracies were eliminated or until I heard from you . . . If you feel that the article even in its corrected and emended form should not appear, I'll, of course, understand and respect your wishes . . .

Greene replied:

I am afraid my memory of the inaccuracies is rather weak."
After the strenuousness of his objections, this lapse stunned
me, as did his lack of interest in refreshing his memory. He
limited himself to commenting, "It wasn't that I had never
met Fidel but you gave the impression I had seen him several times. I had one interview with him that lasted from
ten in the evening till about three in the morning! Yes, An-
tigua was wrong. The black Greene family, if it exists, is in
St. Kitts. With the corrections made I have no objections to
the article appearing if you are getting some money out of
it. If you are not getting some money from it, I suggest you
use me as a bogey to stop it.

Playboy lost interest when it learned that I would have to
revise and edit the profile, and that I expected to be paid.

In 1986, as I assembled a collection of articles that I had
published over the past twenty years, I once again invited
Greene to read the profile and identify its errors. He repeated
that he had faint recall of the mistakes and allowed the piece
to be included in *Playing Away*.

In fairness, it's worth noting that he was preoccupied
during this period with other matters. He regularly visited
Panama to research a book about Omar Torrijos. (It later appeared under the title *Getting to Know the General*.) He attended the signing of the Panama Canal treaty in Washington, D.C., traveling with Torrijo's entourage. He and Gabriel
García Márquez served as negotiators in a couple of kidnapping cases in Central America. So it's understandable that the
particulars of the profile had slipped his mind.

Then again, maybe the shortcomings of the piece had never deserved the kind of blistering criticism he had leveled at it. He may actually have enjoyed my muddying the vast reservoir of dubious anecdotes about him.

As our relationship resumed, it wasn't Greene's style to explain or apologize, but he confided that with age he suffered fewer and fewer mood swings. No manic highs, no suicidal lows as in the past. To demonstrate the present smoothness of his disposition, he attempted to draw a straight line in the air. Because of Dupuytren's contracture, his crooked fingers traced a jagged arc that no amount of effort on his part could flatten out.

IN 1977, LINDA and I and Sean, now a rambunctious two-year-old, occupied the ground-floor apartment of the Villa Chiaraviglio, the most palatial accommodation at the American Academy in Rome. It had a kitchen the size of an amphitheater, a *salone* with a woodburning fireplace, and vaulted ceilings twenty feet high. Double doors opened in the rear onto a brick terrace, and beyond it a garden of lemon and orange trees and shrubs that a team of topiary artists pruned into ovals, pyramids, and obelisks.

The property abutted the rear of the Fontana dell'Acqua Paola, which architecture books describe as "the Baroque at its most serene and loving." Viewed from the esplanade in front of the fountain, the city seemed somnolently untouched by time. The same church domes and cupolas that appear in Piranesi's eighteenth-century prints still punctuate the skyline.

But Rome's peaceful appearance was deceiving. Soon after we arrived, *Newsweek* ran a cover feature, "Living in Anarchy," that decried Italy's violent street crime and the tide of political bloodshed. It illustrated the text with snapshots of police in riot gear, armed guerrillas masked by red bandannas, and wounded and dead bodies splashed against pristine white marble.

The radical poet Nanni Balestrini dubbed this era *Anni di piombo*, the Years of Lead. Underground activists declared war against the state and terrorists rampaged through the city, kidnapping, kneecapping, and killing prominent people. The Red Brigades systematically set out to provoke an overreaction from the government, waving banners that read TANTO PEGGIO, TANTO MEGLIO—the worse it gets, the better it gets. In their clotted revolutionary jargon, "Violence is the coagulant of the movement's subjective energy."

As for my own "subjective energy," it fed on daily doses of tumult and catastrophe. Like Greene, I felt energized "on the dangerous edge of things." The idea of a book about Wayne Dresbach, my childhood friend who murdered his parents, had long been on my mind. Paroled after twelve years in prison, he flew to Rome, living with me, Linda, and Sean in the Villa Chiaraviglio while I tape-recorded hours of interviews with him. In his free time, he crossed the street to the American Academy and played pool with that year's batch of Fellows. When an architect from the University of Utah asked what institution he was affiliated with, Wayne said, "Patuxent Institute for Defective Delinquents." After that, some Fellows started to keep their distance. One night while Wayne babysat Sean, Linda and I went to dinner with friends who became apoplectic with worry that we had left our son with a convicted killer. That ended the evening prematurely and Linda and I tramped home over cobblestone streets staring up at the splendid ceilings of grand palazzi that gleamed with murals of angels and saints. At home, Wayne had changed Sean into his pajamas and was reading him a bedtime story while drinking a beer.

The cognitive dissonance between the image of Italy in bloody shambles and its postcard pictures called to mind the country's Janus face, perpetually gazing in opposite directions. The walls all around us were runed over with menacing graffiti: THE MACHINE GUN IS BEAUTIFUL, AMERICANS, YOU WILL RETURN HOME IN CASKETS. Along the Tiber River embankment somebody had had the leisure to scribble letters ten feet tall: AS LONG AS THE VIOLENCE OF THE STATE IS CALLED JUSTICE, THE JUSTICE OF THE PROLETARIAT WILL BE CALLED VIOLENCE.

Then on a cold morning in March 1978, at a flower-bedecked intersection on Monte Mario, the Red Brigades mowed down Aldo Moro's bodyguards and kidnapped the country's former prime minister and most prominent politician. While they held Moro hostage and demanded the release of prisoners, I received a call from an editor at the *New York Times*, a woman I had once had dinner with as we spitballed ideas for articles I might one day do for her. She wanted a piece now about the Red Brigades. Not the standard pablum based on slightly refined gossip and rumors recycled from the undependable Italian press. She wanted a groundbreaking, eyewitness account from inside a terrorist cell. She wanted me to show the human face behind the mask.

I laughed. What she suggested was a sick joke in which any mention of a kill fee amounted to bleak black humor. Not a single antiterrorist agent from any nation's intelligence service had penetrated a Red Brigades *covo*. Several investigative journalists imagined they had arranged underground interviews, only to have their kneecaps blown off. One brave hack had been shot point-blank and left to die in front of his wife.

None of this dissuaded the *Times* editor. "That's the beauty of it," she said. "It's never been done before. You do it and a newspaper article is the least of what you'll get out of it. There's bound to be a book contract and a movie deal."

"Why not give this assignment to your Rome correspondent?" I asked, well aware that Henry Kamm would howl in derision at the notion that he risk his life on such a foolhardy mission.

"Don't say no, Mike, until you think this through and check your sources in Rome."

"My sources could recommend a good restaurant. Nothing more."

"All the years you've lived there, you must know someone who could introduce you to someone else who could put you in touch with the right person."

"I wouldn't have a clue where to start."

After a prolonged silence, the *Times* editor posed a tantalizing question. "Who knows any more about the Red Brigades than you do?"

I don't remember how I answered. What I remember is thinking that she seemed to imply that nobody knew enough about the Red Brigades to contradict anything I wrote.

For fifty-four days her question clattered in my head just like helicopters clattered over the city, launching futile raids on suspected safe houses where they never found Aldo Moro. In my imagination I ran with the Red Brigades and rode shotgun with the *carabinieri* and felt close to Moro in captivity. On sunny afternoons, Sean and I gamboled through the gardens of the Villa Chiaraviglio playing a game we called Searching for Mister Moro.

On May 9, on a humid overcast afternoon, I caught a bus from the Gianicolo down through Trastevere to the Ponte Garibaldi, where traffic stopped dead. I assumed a demonstration had paralyzed the area, and for fifteen minutes I gazed through the grimy window at the Tiber River, green as a snakeskin. Finally, growing impatient, I climbed down from the bus into a mass of people murmuring a single word. "Moro," they whispered. "Moro, Moro."

In the Jewish Quarter, I gathered information as I body-surfed through the crowd. Moro's corpse had been discovered in the trunk of a Renault parked on Via Michelangelo Caetani. For fear the Renault was booby-trapped, the *carabinieri* tried to clear the street before processing the crime scene.

I pressed forward, through the maze of medieval alleys, some little more than an arm-span wide. At Piazza Mattei, there was a fountain where naked bronze boys hoisted bronze turtles into a pond. At a police checkpoint, I flashed my credentials for the upcoming Italian Open tennis tournament. The card was stenciled in block letters STAMPA, meaning press. Without a second glance, the cops waved me onto Via Caetani, where a priest was bent over Moro's body, administering the last rites.

Contemporary news accounts and subsequent books claimed that Moro had been deposited equidistant between the Communist Party's and the Christian Democratic Party's headquarters as a gesture of contempt to both ends of the political spectrum. But in fact the Renault was abandoned across from the entrance to the American Studies Center. If there was any symbolism, it was more likely a condemnation of U.S. intrusions into Italian affairs.

Once the priest finished, I stayed on and watched the forensic team work. I felt sure Graham Greene—that any novelist worthy of the name—would have done the same. With a splinter of ice in my heart, I stared into the Renault's open trunk. It wasn't a pretty sight. But my childhood had been good preparation for this moment. It was no worse than the automobile accidents my mother had taken me to on the Washington–Baltimore Parkway.

Attracted by the crowd, indifferent to the propinquity of death, a vendor plunked down buckets of olives in brine and garbanzo beans in oil, ready for business. The *carabinieri* chased him off. They had tears in their eyes. So did many mourners in the crowd. As Moro's body was removed, people with armfuls of flowers arrived and arranged a tribute that has ever since been sporadically replenished.

I recalled the conversation I had had with the *New York Times* editor. It clung to me like a burr, prickly and provocative. That evening I started jotting down notes for a novel about a journalist who, under financial duress, agrees to write a book from inside a terrorist cell. All the while he intends to pass off fiction as fact, and concocts a plot, the kidnapping of Aldo Moro, that mirrors the Red Brigades' plan.

XII

~~~~~~~~~~~~~

AFTER A YEAR in Europe, the return to Texas always doubled me over like a case of the bends. No matter how cautiously I eased back into Austin and academia, I felt I had surfaced too fast. The September heat was Saharan, English departmental politics Machiavellian.

Linda and I sublet, sight unseen, a paint-peeling house that the owners described by mail as a renovated nineteenth-century carpenter's Gothic mansion. We arrived to discover the renovations half-finished, with the exterior as decrepit as that of the Hotel Oloffson in Haiti and the interior rooms stripped to bare wood, like a jumble of discarded crates. Because the ground floor had no heat, we huddled all winter upstairs, as uncomfortable as we had been anyplace else during our dozen years of marriage.

Still, we weren't unhappy there. Sean, as I wrote to Graham Greene, "frequently swipes my pens and scribbles on paper and proudly proclaims 'I writer.' Poor deluded kid. We were so hoping he'd go into law or medicine or real estate and be able to support us."

Another cause for pleasure, Philip Mayer paid us a surprise visit. He had flown to America out of curiosity about the State of the Nation, which he satisfied the hard way by riding Greyhound buses across the continent and filing articles for the *Irish Times*. Despite his diabetes, he blithely accepted the dangers of the trip, flopping in fleabag motels and eating at truck stops. On several occasions, as he injected his insulin, he was accosted by cops who threatened to arrest him until he convinced them he wasn't a junkie.

With the proceeds from the sale of Montclair, Philip had bought a two-bedroom apartment in La Bocca, near Cannes. He said it would be empty for much of July and welcomed us to stay there.

Before we left Austin, the *New Yorker* published a long profile of Graham Greene. Naturally it nettled me that they had accepted this piece, not mine, which had been submitted to them two years earlier. I knew, however, that the *New Yorker* preferred to use its own staff writers. So it didn't surprise me that the assignment had gone to Penelope Gilliatt, the magazine's film critic and a respected novelist and screenwriter, best known for *Sunday, Bloody Sunday*.

From its opening paragraph, Gilliatt's "The Dangerous Edge" had my fingerprints all over it. Among the similarities to "The Staying Power and the Glory," Gilliatt quoted Greene lamenting his noisy neighbors who barbecued on their balconies, ruining his sleep. Gilliatt described Greene as tall, six feet, two inches. "He bends his head a little not in the stoop of age but in attention, so as to lose nothing." That sounded close to my description of Greene as "tall, well over six feet . . . if he does stoop slightly at the shoulder, it's not as if bowed by years but as though to incline an ear and listen closer."

I drew up a list, comparing Gilliatt's article to mine, laying out passages side by side. Sometimes Gilliatt quoted my piece verbatim, without attribution. At other times she borrowed phrases and recombined them. Over and over again, there were echoes of my work, some subtle, many more ringingly loud. She remarked that Greene "used to write five hundred words a day, stopping, if necessary, in the middle of a sentence." During our discussion of his work habits, Greene told me his daily production had declined to a hundred words and "[s]ometimes I stop smack in the middle of a paragraph."

Gilliatt remarked that Greene created characters "who have to be strong because they are weak, who have to be good because they think themselves sinners." This was strikingly like my observation about Greene's characters "who have to be strong because they know they are weak, who are good because they are sinners."

The final paragraph of Gilliatt's profile was a purée of my work, piecing together fragments and in one case repeating a quote from Greene that he had denied making to me. "I have no talent. It's just a question of working, of being willing to put in the time."

I worried that Greene would erupt in anger again and protest that "The Staying Power and the Glory" had now spread misinformation about him to a wider audience. I phoned Owen Laster, who reminded me he was my agent, not a lawyer. He wasn't qualified to advise me about legalities of plagiarism and he had no stomach for tangling with the *New Yorker*. Plenty of his clients were dying to appear in its pages. If he became involved in my case, he feared the *New Yorker* would never do another dollar's worth of business with him. Was I, he asked, willing to alienate such a prestigious magazine so early in my career?

When I contacted *The Nation*, the original U.S. publisher of the Greene profile, they sounded bemused at being plagiarized by a commercial powerhouse like the *New Yorker*. A small liberal journal with a reputation for punching above its weight, *The Nation* had no appetite for this fight. They feared that legal bills would bankrupt them, and encouraged me to take solace from the old adage that imitation is the sincerest form of flattery.

Next I reached out to Gloria Emerson, whom I had introduced to Graham Greene when she needed help to arrange an interview with him for *Rolling Stone*. Gloria referred to me as Misha, as if I were a raw Russian youth. Twenty-five years my senior, she alternated between mothering me and disciplining me. The day I called for advice she was in a disciplinary mood. "Oh, Misha, don't make a big deal of this. We all borrow from one another."

Perplexed and not a little suspicious, I tracked down her piece in *Rolling Stone*. Sure enough, Gloria had opened it with Greene in his apartment in Antibes, protesting that his neighbors ruined his sleep with their late-night barbecues. She also repeated the anecdote about the CIA warning Greene every night in Santiago that they were watching him. Greene had vehemently denied he ever received such a call and accused me of sloppy reporting. With neither the energy nor the financial resources to pursue a second claim of plagiarism, I didn't speak to Gloria Emerson again until shortly before she committed suicide, having written her own obituary in advance.

Finally I consulted an attorney in Austin, an affable fellow who had drawn up my will. Examining the parallel passages, he said it appeared to him that Penelope Gilliatt was guilty of plagiarism, but a lot depended on whether my piece had been copyrighted. And had Gilliatt stolen enough to constitute copyright infringement? What kind of compensatory damages could I demand after *The Nation* and *London Magazine* had paid me a pittance? The *New Yorker*'s legal department might argue I deserved at most a small permissions fee and no punitive damages.

To win a substantial settlement, the lawyer explained, I would have to prove that the *New Yorker* had appropriated my material with foreknowledge and reckless disregard for my proprietary rights. Although he would be happy to represent me, he asked for a ten-thousand-dollar retainer. Seeing my shoulders slump, he recommended that I show the *New Yorker* the parallel passages and count on the magazine to do the decent thing.

Not wholly without hope, I drafted a letter to William Shawn, the longtime editor of the *New Yorker*, who had a reputation for fair play and civility, qualities that had grown increasingly rare in the hurly-burly publishing business. Universally referred to as Mister Shawn, he had, I assumed, never heard of me. So I reminded him that the *New Yorker* had reviewed two of my novels positively, and added that I trusted we could amicably resolve this problem.

I was accustomed to dilatory editors who sometimes didn't bother to acknowledge article proposals, much less random letters. But Mister Shawn speedily replied, phoning me in Austin. When Linda told him I was out of town, he called me at a friend's house in Houston. His voice had a reassuring pastoral resonance, and he expressed his regret in homiletic sentences. He didn't quibble over the parallel passages I had sent him. He conceded there were similarities and in some cases direct quotes. He defined the issue as "unconscious plagiarism" on Penelope Gilliatt's part.

MICHAEL MEWSHAW

As if confiding secrets to a professional acquaintance, he revealed that despite her distinguished career, Ms. Gilliatt had long been plagued by emotional troubles; she suffered from alcoholism and an unnamed drug dependence. When she reviewed movies for the *New Yorker*, the magazine assigned a minder to make sure she got the plot straight.

This had all been very unpleasant, Mister Shawn said, for the *New Yorker*, not to mention for him and now for me. Despite the fabled reputation of the magazine's fact-checking department, he claimed that the incident had caught everybody off guard. If I would be good enough to tell him what I wanted, he would consider what should be done.

My initial anger had faded under the influence of Mister Shawn's mellifluous voice. Still, I was firm about my demands—a public acknowledgment in the magazine and financial compensation. What do you usually pay for long profiles? I asked.

"That depends. There's no set fee. We take into account the author's seniority, the newsworthiness of the subject, and, of course, the quality of the finished product."

"I'd like to be paid whatever Ms. Gilliatt got," I said.

"I'm afraid that's confidential. I'm willing to pay you a thousand dollars. As for publishing an acknowledgment, Ms. Gilliatt's in a precarious state of mind. Public humiliation might lead her to do something self-destructive. With highstrung writers, I always fear the possibility of suicide."

I wasn't heartless. I refused to haggle if a life hung in the balance. It was only years later I learned that Mister Shawn had a penchant for raising the problem of suicide whenever he felt backed into a corner. Lillian Ross, his mistress for decades, recalled in her autobiography, *Here But Not Here: A Love*

163

Story, that Mister Shawn refused to marry her, saying that he feared his wife would kill herself.

"This is a moral choice," Mister Shawn told me. "It's up to you and your conscience. If you'll compromise on a public acknowledgment, I'll double the money."

Although I had no idea of the *New Yorker*'s pay scale, I suspected Ms. Gilliatt had pocketed more than two thousand dollars for her—for my!—profile. But I didn't care to have her death, much less Mister Shawn's priestly disapproval, on my conscience. So I accepted his offer and insisted that he guarantee that the piece would never appear in any *New Yorker* anthology or collection of Ms. Gilliatt's work.

"Of course," Mister Shawn agreed. "You've made the moral choice, Mr. Mewshaw. I really don't think she knew what she was doing."

Within days a check for two thousand dollars arrived, along with a cover letter signed by William Shawn: "Thank you for your extraordinary kindness in withdrawing your request for a public acknowledgment. We, in turn, will not ever grant permission to any publication or publishing house, or the author, to reprint the Graham Greene Profile."

WHILE LINDA, SEAN, and I were in Europe that summer, information reached me in dribs and drabs revealing the depths of Mister Shawn's duplicity. Whereas he had told me he had been blindsided by the problem with Penelope Gilliatt's article, Greene had already written the *New Statesman* that readers should place no trust in her "so-called Profile. . . . It will be safer for them to assume that almost anything I am made to say is probably—to put it politely—inaccurate. Her imagina-

tion extends from recording the presence of vultures in Antibes to a mysterious Czech official of the Ministry of Foreign
Affairs who, she writes, abused me on BBC . . . An even more
mysterious Englishman apparently invited me to visit an in-
ternment camp in Argentina, but I'm afraid both the camp
and the Englishman are products of Ms. Gilliatt's rather wild
imagination."

I was relieved that Greene's objections to the Gilliatt profile had not mentioned any of his criticisms of my piece in *The
Nation*. Was he doing me a favor? Or had he forgotten his
heated criticisms?

Despite her supposedly poor health, Gilliatt offered a pep-
py defense of herself to Herbert Mitgang, of the *New York
Times*. She characterized the letter to the *New Statesman* as
leg-pulling "typical of Greene's sense of humor." She called
him "a most witty and convivial man—I believe we understand each other."

That was the last time Ms. Gilliatt publicly addressed the
issue. The *New Yorker* announced that she had taken a medical leave of absence. In the following years, she contributed the
occasional short story but never again published nonfiction in
the magazine.

Mister Shawn declared to the press that she "doesn't think
she made mistakes." Fact checkers, he insisted, had verified
that vultures did exist in Antibes. He assured Herbert Mitgang "that the [Greene] profile had gone through the usual
checking procedures and no red flags had been raised." When
Mitgang asked about my complaints, Mister Shawn said,
"[N]o plagiarism suit had been contemplated" and claimed that
I withdrew my request for an acknowledgment when I learned
of Ms. Gilliatt's fragile state of mind.

I contacted Mitgang and asked why he hadn't allowed me to speak for myself. He said he had looked up my phone number in the New York City directory but hadn't found a listing. Apparently, it didn't occur to him that some writers don't reside in the 212 area code. As for correcting the record now, Mitgang pleaded that he had no desire to gang up on Penelope Gilliatt and revisit the subject.

But employees at the *New Yorker* soon began ganging up on Mister Shawn. Perhaps this was inevitable. He had aged without anointing a successor, and there were grievances among staff members competing to replace him. It emerged that Ms. Gilliatt had plagiarized another author in her Graham Greene profile. Judith Adamson, an expert on Greene's film career, protested that the *New Yorker* had used her research without attribution. Once again Mister Shawn refused to publish an acknowledgment but paid a financial settlement.

He managed to hold on to the editorship until the *New Yorker* was purchased by Advance Publications. No great respecter of reputations or traditions, S. I. Newhouse, Advance's chairman, forced Mister Shawn out in 1987. Upon Mister Shawn's death, in 1992, obituaries and eulogies sounded bright notes in a chorus of praise for a legendary literary figure, a man said to have been shy but resolute, candid yet infinitely courteous.

Eventually, however, a less flattering portrait of Mister Shawn emerged. In her memoir, *Gone: The Last Days of the New Yorker*, Renata Adler, a former staff writer and a member of Mister Shawn's inner circle, described the earthquake caused in-house by the Graham Greene profile. "Over the years, Mr. Shawn had several times been put on notice that Ms. Gilliatt plagiarized. In this instance the checkers had noticed that Ms.

Gilliatt's piece tracked, to an extraordinary degree, an article in *The Nation* by Michael Mewshaw. They had called this to Mr. Shawn's attention. He called it to the attention of Ms. Gilliatt. She was incensed. Of course, she said, Graham Greene had said to Mr. Mewshaw the same sorts of things he said to her—evidence not of plagiarism but of accuracy. This did not quite meet the facts. Her profile tracked Mr. Mewshaw's in details that could not have come from Graham Greene. After a tirade or two from Ms. Gilliatt, Mr. Shawn made his decision. He ran the piece."

Gardner Botsford had joined the *New Yorker* in 1942, and after thirty-seven years on the job, he served alternately as Mister Shawn's right-hand man and his whipping boy. According to Mr. Botsford's memoir, *A Privileged Life Mostly*, the relationship between them had by 1979 sunk to a low ebb.

"The wretched Penelope Gilliatt mess," Botsford wrote, "put the magazine in a serious pickle, and Shawn himself in a worse one . . . Her profile of Graham Greene, edited by Shawn himself, had just appeared and its publication was quickly followed by a letter from Michael Mewshaw, who demonstrated that she had lifted, untouched, whole paragraphs from an article on Greene he had written for the *New Republic* [sic]. This was bad enough, but then it developed that Peter Canby, the *New Yorker*'s checker, had detected the plagiarism and had sent Shawn a proof identifying the purloined passages . . . Shawn's personal pickle was that he could deny nothing: he had seen the Canby proof—he had written notes and queries on it in his own tiny handwriting—and put the Profile to press anyway. Mewshaw's letter and Canby's proof had been seen by a number of staff members in the course of their normal duties, and thus, inevitably, by the staff at large, which meant, in due course, the outside world heard all about it too. Newspaper reporters from the *New York Times* and the *Washington Post* called me for comment, and so did Pauline Kael from the West Coast, where she was being badgered by the press. I fended them off for the moment and went to see Shawn and find out what line we should take. He was in a state. He had never been in a bind like this before, and when I mentioned the *Times* and the *Post*, he blew up all over the place. Somehow the train wreck was my fault, and he accused me of using it in an effort to take his job."

In 2020 I discovered that "The Dangerous Edge," Penelope Gilliatt's profile of Graham Greene, was included in the *New Yorker's* online archive in its original form, without any deletion of the material plagiarized from my work. This seemed a blatant violation of the 1979 agreement between Mister Shawn and me. I emailed the magazine, requesting an explanation and an apology. Along with a summary of the original dispute, I sent a copy of Mister Shawn's letter guaranteeing that the *New Yorker* "will never grant permission to any publication or publishing house, or to the author, to reprint the Graham Greene profile."

When an exchange of emails with Deputy Editor Deirdre Foley-Mendelssohn led nowhere, I hired a lawyer, who cautioned me that the Condé Nast legal team could be counted on to mount a hardnosed defense. He doubted the *New Yorker* would acknowledge any wrongdoing. The best I could hope for, he said, was that the magazine would remove Gilliatt's article from its website or at least eliminate the material taken from me. He added that he would request a financial settlement.

As predicted, Condé Nast's attorney played hardball. He interpreted Mister Shawn's letter to mean that whereas other magazines and publishers were forbidden to reprint Gilliatt's article, the *New Yorker* was free to do so. While he didn't deny that my work had been used without attribution, he argued that this didn't necessarily constitute a copyright violation or rise to the level of a legal infraction. The *New Yorker* refused to withdraw, or redact parts of, Gilliatt's article.

Instead, it offered to add a prefatory note to the online archive stating that this profile includes quotes, phrases, and observations drawn without attribution from the article "The Staying Power and the Glory," by Michael Mewshaw, published in the April 16, 1977, issue of *The Nation*.

Fed up with communicating through a picket fence of lawyers, I emailed David Remnick, the current *New Yorker* editor, directly and suggested we settle the matter in person. I urged him to recall that I had "accepted in good faith what had been offered to me [by Mister Shawn] in bad faith." I made "a moral choice" while not in possession of all the "facts." Now I urged him "to make a moral choice. Unlike Mister Shawn I'm asking this of you with no hidden agenda and the facts in full daylight."

Remnick replied that he understood my distress and was sensitive to my concerns. But he wouldn't budge on the bottom line.

My first instinct was to fight until the last round and force the *New Yorker* to concede it had treated me shabbily in the past and was doing so again. But on reflection I recognized that the *New Yorker* was unwittingly doing me a favor. If it had simply deleted Penelope Gilliatt's plagiarized profile, the entire episode would have sunk without a trace. But by inserting a prefatory statement, it was reminding the public of a less than admirable moment in the *New Yorker*'s history, and by paying my legal expenses it was, as lawyers put it, making me whole.

XIII

⟨⟩⟨⟩⟨⟩⟨⟩⟨⟩⟨⟩⟨⟩

EARFUL THAT THE Penelope Gilliatt imbroglio might
put Greene and me at odds again, I rang his flat in Antibes, then his apartment in Paris, then his house in Capri.
When I got no answer, I called his French agent, Michelle
Lapautre, who also represented me. She said Greene was
driving around Spain with Father Duran, and she either
couldn't or wouldn't tell me his reaction to the *New Yorker*
contretemps.

Back in Texas and teaching full time, I focused on *Life for
Death*, my first book of nonfiction, and months slipped by. It
wasn't until March 1980, that I broke a long silence:

Dear Graham,

The *New Statesman* called and asked me to review *Doctor
Fischer of Geneva*. After considerable reflection I agreed to
do it. And I'm glad I did. Both Linda and I enjoyed the
book immensely. It seemed to me your best work in years—
taut, finely crafted, concise, yet fully realized.

I've been meaning to write you for almost a year. I wanted to tell you that even before I knew you had objected to Penelope Gilliatt's profile in the *New Yorker*, I had written them to say that she had plagiarized from my article which I later learned from you was inaccurate.

I understand perfectly now why you dislike being interviewed. Actually I've come to have deep misgivings about the entire field of journalism. Almost every experience I've had with it has been bad.

That aside, we are well. Tomorrow is my son Sean's fifth birthday. Linda is expecting a baby in mid-June and we're hoping for a girl.

As I waited for an answer, I wondered whether Greene regarded me as a leper without a bell, the kind of innocent he described in *The Quiet American* as tainting everything he touched. But he replied:

Forgive the long delay in answering your letter but I have been away in England attending the rehearsals of a play [*For Whom the Bell Chimes*]. I am delighted to hear that you are reviewing *Dr. Fischer* in the *New Statesman*, though I await your review with some trepidation.

Yes, I heard that you were involved in that appalling profile by Penelope Gilliatt. I think the poor woman was half off her head. Drugs or drink or both.

Congratulations on the new baby and may it be a girl . . . I hope that one day you will return to these parts so that we can see all of you together.

Almost immediately I had to apologize to Greene again.

"The review [of *Dr. Fischer*] as it was printed was not the one I wrote. I was asked for 1,300 words, but the *New Statesman* deleted several sentences without consulting me in advance or explaining afterward." I enclosed a copy of the original review, which conveyed far more of my enthusiasm.

Greene assured me the review was fine as printed and that literary journals were always pressed for space and often had no time to consult reviewers. He added, "I received *Life for Death* and was very impressed by it . . . What about trying the Bodley Head? Have they turned it down? It's absurd if they have as it's a most sellable book."

There are countless stories about Greene's chilly detachment and his outbursts of cruelty. His cousin Barbara, who accompanied him on his trek through Liberia, wrote in her account of the journey, "[A]part from three or four people he was really fond of, I felt that the rest of humanity was to [Greene] like a heap of insects that he liked to examine . . . coldly and clearly." Yet except for his outrage over my article, he was never anything except kind and supportive to me.

I wrote to him that Linda and I were jittery as the baby's birth drew near:

> On Monday we were upset to hear that Linda's mother had fallen down a flight of steps and broken her ribs, her wrist, and a vertebra in her neck. Miraculously, she will be all right. But then today Linda learned she may have to have the baby by caesarean section and we're still trying to assimilate that news. The doctor says it's nothing to worry about, but it does little to reduce our tension.

Greene responded promptly:

I hope all goes well with Linda and that your suspense will soon be over. My former girlfriend had three caesareans, one of which produced twins and she suffered no ill affects [sic]. However I won't wish twins on you.

I scrawled:

. . . a hasty note at this hectic time to thank you for your letter and to tell you everything turned out well. Once Linda went into labor, things moved with startling quickness. We arrived at the hospital at 4:20 a.m. and the baby arrived at 4:31 a.m.—feet first. There was no time for a caesarean, no time for an anesthetic, barely time for Linda to take off her clothes. It was a boy, 6 lb. 8 oz. We're calling him Marc . . .

Now Marc and Linda are home and we're trying to establish some sort of routine—one which will be broken a month from now when we leave Texas, drive east and prepare to move to Rome in October. At the moment I think we'd be willing to go anywhere to escape the heat. For weeks the temperature has hovered near 100 degrees.

Greene replied:

All my congratulations on the quick birth to you and Linda. It's a good thing to escape a caesarean. The awful heat, which I've been reading about in the newspapers, can't have made things easier.

It's good that you are coming again to Europe . . . my love to the enlarged family.

I could never count on such sentiments from my family. The day Marc was born, I called home to announce that Linda and the baby were recovering nicely. In a dead, cold voice that I had dreaded since childhood, my mother asked, "Are you sitting down?"

"What's wrong?"

"Your book. That's what's wrong." Months before its publication, she had checked the manuscript of *Life for Death* and had expressed no objections. Now she had plenty.

"What gives you the right," she demanded, "to spread around my private business?"

"The book's about Wayne, not you."

"But you write that I was divorced."

"That's a tiny part of the book. Nobody'll notice."

"I noticed!"

"Mom, be reasonable. You read the book. That was the time to complain. Not now. Not the day of your grandson's birth."

"Don't tell me when I can or can't speak. Just hear me now. I never want to see you again. Not ever! Don't call. Don't write." She smashed the receiver onto its cradle.

My status as family pariah persisted until shortly before our departure for Italy. A CAT scan revealed a lesion on my mother's lung. A lifelong smoker, she had good reason to fear she had cancer. Before she was operated on, she summoned me to her hospital bedside for a reconciliation. When the tumor turned out to be benign, she survived for two more decades, and we repeated this minuet many times. I would be banished, then reembraced, then banished again. When she actually was on her deathbed and I asked to visit, she refused to see me.

IN ROME, I improvised an office on the living room couch and wrote in a spiral notebook propped on my lap. Marc lay on a pillow beside me, a colicky baby prone to catching every cold and flu Sean carried home from kindergarten. The woodburning fireplace provided a bit of cheer and the scent of pine cones, but little heat. Every time I got up to stoke the embers, the baby started crying.

After Christmas, we transferred from the baronial Villa Chiaraviglio to a cottage on the American Academy grounds constructed atop an electrical generator. On the façade a sign warned PERICOLO DI MORTE. Danger of Death. I didn't take this seriously until one morning as I showered the hot-water heater exploded and a fork of lightning sizzled up one of my arms and down the other.

Then, almost as shocking, a manila envelope festooned with official stamps and seals reached me from the University of Texas. Inside the envelope a slightly smaller one bore the return address of a law firm in Washington, D.C. Because of the crush of holiday mail and the waywardness of the Italian postal service, a libel suit against me had spent more than a month slow-poking across the Atlantic Ocean. Legally the notice was supposed to be served on me in person, but the English Department secretary had signed for it, and by the time the papers were in my hands, I was already in default.

The plaintiff, Lee Dresbach, Wayne's younger brother and my foster brother, the fellow who had lived with my family for years, took strenuous exception to *Life for Death*. Accusing me of invasion of privacy and defamation with actual malice, Lee demanded six million dollars in damages.

Our abrupt decision to leave Rome had nothing to do with the lawsuit. We wanted to flee the Danger of Death house and find a more salubrious climate for Marc, whose respiratory problems had become chronic. The *Daily American*, Italy's English-language newspaper, ran an ad for a traditional *carmen* style house constructed around a courtyard in Granada, Spain. Dealing long distance with the owner, we agreed to a three-month lease.

Because we had accumulated several cubic yards of toys, on top of boxes of books and clothes, we rented a Fiat from Avis and packed it to the rafters with our belongings. I drove to Spain. Linda planned to follow with the boys by plane. But by the time I hit the autostrada to Florence, I had a headache. In Genoa, I started sniffling and sneezing. At the French border, I began coughing, and when I pitched up at Philip Mayer's apartment in La Bocca, I was suffering a 103° fever.

Certain I was contagious, I suggested staying at a hotel, but Philip and Claire wouldn't hear of it. They bedded me down in a spare room and for the next three days fed me soup, cough syrup, and aspirin. Still weak, I protested that I had to be on my way. They argued that I shouldn't drive alone. Philip volunteered to keep me company as far as Marseilles, where he would catch a return train.

But we sped through Marseilles without slowing down. We were not only making good time, but we were also having a good time, trading stories about how we met our wives, what we hoped for our kids, and what I should expect in Spain, which had just survived an attempted coup. I confessed to Philip my worries about Lee Dresbach's lawsuit and my fears that I was asking too much of Linda with the unstable life I imposed on her.

Philip argued that I misperceived my situation. "After a rough start in life," he said, "you've reached liftoff." With his hand, he traced a rocket's steep trajectory. "The hardest part was getting off the ground. Now that you're airborne, don't even consider taking your foot off the accelerator."

When we made it as far as Montpellier, he told me to skip the train station. He had decided to stay there overnight. After buying a toothbrush and razor, he phoned Claire with the excuse that I was still shaky and needed company.

In the morning I felt hoarse, but couldn't say whether this was a lingering side effect of the flu or the aftermath of our nonstop talking. At breakfast, we somehow segued to the Arab–Israeli conflict, a subject about which Philip, a Jew, had strong opinions.

Once we finished our coffee—we never finished the discussion—Philip debated whether to catch the noon train to Cannes. "But why bother?" he said. "There'll be better connections from Barcelona. We'll be there in a few hours."

We might well have been if we hadn't stopped to fill up with gas. The grease monkey who manned the station somehow got it in his head—he looked to be high on diesel fumes—that I had stolen money from the cash register as I came back from the toilet. He ripped the key out of the Fiat's ignition and refused to let us leave until I paid him back. Philip suggested we call the police and have them sort this out. My suggestion was to knock the guy to the garage floor and grab the key.

"No, no," Philip protested. "That's the Arab–Israeli way of dealing with problems. Don't negotiate, just bomb. You need to defuse the tension." He urged the grease monkey to count the till and check whether anything was missing. Once the man satisfied himself that he hadn't been robbed, he allowed us to drive on.

We rolled into Barcelona just about dinnertime as reckoned by a Spanish body clock. After we registered at a hotel on the Rambla and garaged the Fiat to prevent thieves from stealing Marc's crib and Sean's precious *Star Wars* toys, it was nearly eleven o'clock and we were lucky to land a table at Los Caracoles, a restaurant on the heaving streets of the Barrio Gótico. Philip loved being in a different country. Though he feared it wouldn't last, he hoped Europe would stay like this, each country, each city, each province with its distinctive culture.

The next day, while Philip was checking the train schedule to France, I heard that President Ronald Reagan had been shot by a madman eager to impress the actress Jodie Foster. Under the circumstances, Philip said, we couldn't separate now: "As my tribe would put it, we have to discuss how this will affect the Jews."

Philip called Claire and explained that he planned to buy fresh underwear and socks and travel south with me. The trip was taking on the trappings of an epic voyage, a variation on "Ithaka," by C. P. Cavafy, full of detours and discoveries: "Arriving there is what you're destined for. / But don't hurry the journey."

I spoke to Linda in Rome and gave her a report on our non-progress. At this rate, I'd be older and wiser upon my arrival in Granada. And as it turned out, richer too. Linda delivered the thrilling news that I had won a Guggenheim—twenty thousand bucks, enough to hold our nostrils above water for another year in Europe.

Philip was as delighted as I was, and as we negotiated the craggy Costa Brava, we chewed over the implications of the grant. The Guggenheim Foundation fancies its award as conferring the equivalent of intellectual knighthood. Although I didn't buy that, Philip urged me to allow that this was a sign that I was on my way. The journey would continue, he said. The point was to stay in the game and keep going.

That night we stopped in Murcia, a city where desertification had singed the surrounding countryside into a replica of the American Southwest. Italian spaghetti westerns were shot in nearby *barrancas* where false-front clapboard villages had been hammered together.

Philip and I ate a celebratory dinner, washed down by a good bottle of Rioja. Though I begged him to join me for the final one hundred and fifty miles to Granada, he decided to turn back and couldn't be persuaded to change his mind. Maybe he feared that the destination, our personal Ithaca, would prove to be a disappointment. Or perhaps he thought it fitting for me to cover the last stretch on my own.

In the morning when I woke, he had already caught a taxi to the train station, leaving me a note thanking me for the ride, as if he, not I, owed a debt of gratitude. He described himself as "a rich man, poor in friends. You don't know how much I've enjoyed this."

SETTLING IN GRANADA, I sent Greene our new address:

When I last wrote from Rome I mentioned we might be moving to the South of France for a few months and I hoped we could have lunch or a drink at least. But fate intervened in the form of a $6 million libel and invasion of privacy suit . . . As you know only too well from your experience with Shirley Temple, this sort of thing is no joke.

For the last few months I've spent much of my time talking long distance to agent, editor, and lawyers.

The upshot is that my royalties for *Life for Death* have been frozen, the American paperback postponed and the English edition delayed until the case has been resolved. I'm supposed to give my deposition in July and then go to trial at the end of September. My first thought is that I have nothing to wear. I don't own a suit or a tie. It'll cost me a fortune to outfit myself to make an impression on the jury.

Perhaps the same outfit will come in handy when I confront bill collectors. I've been advised that my part of the legal fees should amount to twice my original advance.

Oh well, I don't want to think about that or about the possibility of losing the case. I'd rather concentrate on my new novel—the story of an American journalist who's writing an altogether fraudulent book about the Red Brigades.

Greene attempted to boost my morale:

I am sorry indeed to hear of your trouble over the legal action. No libel action in the United States seems to be for less than several million dollars which makes me more glad than ever that I don't live there! It's a shocking thing that this should have interfered with your publication in England of *Life for Death* which seems to me your best book to date. Do let me know how things go eventually.

"Eventually" proved to be farther off than I feared. It would be more than a year before my legal situation was settled. Meanwhile, we did our best to enjoy life in Andalusia.

Tucked away in the Albaicín, Granada's ancient Arab quarter, our house had breath-catching views of the Alhambra and the Sierra Nevada in the distance. Every day as the snow receded a bit more on the mountain peaks, the temperature rose in town and Marc's sniffles gradually dried up. Sean played in the plaza with neighborhood kids who taught him to cuss in the local dialect and beg pesetas from tourists. A gardener supplied us with strawberries, and a maid who came with the *carmen* prepared gazpacho, which we drank by the gallon, as if it were Gatorade. In a tower above the master bedroom, I worked on the new novel, and while I never forgot that the meter was running and legal bills were piling up in the States, I rejoiced in being where I was.

We considered staying in Spain for the duration of the Guggenheim grant, but in autumn we headed back to Rome, where a different debate began. For years, we had been nibbling at the subject like a couple of fish with a scrap of bait. Now we bit down to its core. Why not cut bait with Texas and stay in Italy?

The idea, I realized in lucid moments, was sheer madness. I was thirty-eight years old, married, with two young children. I had tenure at UT. Why throw away the security, especially with Lee Dresbach's lawsuit bleeding us white?

But the words in Saul Bellow's *The Rain King* haunted me. "I want, I want." I wanted to be a writer, not a professor of writing. I wanted to base myself in Europe as a jumping-off point for novels I planned to set in North Africa and the Middle East. I loathed the idea of becoming a model citizen in Austin, Texas, and wanted to discover a more interesting way of being unhappy. I suppose I had simply never gotten over wanting to be Graham Greene.

LINDA AND I didn't ever consciously decide to become expatriates. We assumed we would eventually return to the States. But for the next decade, we sublet six different apartments in various *rioni* of Rome, never feathering our nest. Despite the admonition of the poet Joseph Brodsky, our Nobel Prize–winning neighbor on the Gianicolo, that there was "no life without furniture," we never bought a stick of the stuff. We restricted our possessions to what we could pack up at a moment's notice and hightail it out of town. Friends joked that we had joined the Witness Protection Program.

This improvised existence seemed to Linda to cast us into jeopardy. Since all our business dealings were in cash, we carried around great wads of lire and looked like those tourists we noticed in the Forum, fretfully slapping at their pants pockets to make sure their wallets were safe.

I was never nearly as anxious as Linda. It seemed to me we inhabited a secret society that welcomed anyone who wised up to its ways. Part of the rush of living in Rome was mastering the ropes and never getting tangled up in red tape. Or else laughing at yourself if you got snared by some dubious law or arcane custom.

Jaded Italians carped that *la dolce vita* was long dead. Still, the country's classic attractions remained—the weather, the food, the wine, the self-contained villages that comprised a metropolis that called itself eternal, yet throbbed with the metabolism of a mayfly. Behind the ornate brocaded tapestry that the city presented to foreigners, Italians pursued their private interests with utter indifference to outsiders. It was in that hidden space where I longed to live.

Graham Greene might have warned me that a hidden space can become a cage, a trap. Yvonne Cloetta remarked in her memoir, "People often call [Greene] the Haunted Man, but he was only haunted by himself, a victim of traps that, unconscious or not, he set up around himself."

It doesn't take much to imagine what Yvonne meant. On the surface Greene appeared to orchestrate his life for maximum freedom—freedom to write, to travel, to sleep around. At some level he seemed to believe in the quote from Joseph Conrad that he used as the epigraph for *The Human Factor*: "I only know that he who forms a tie is lost." By remaining separated but still married to Vivien, he held other women at arm's length, just as he held off his son and daughter. Moving from one mistress to another, he gave the impression of being cold, even heartless. But examined more closely, his attempts to protect himself turned him into a prisoner. Moves he made to liberate himself ended up marooning him in his own misery. Every path he chose had its pitfalls. Every effort to guard his privacy added to his loneliness.

His love life in all its intricacies demonstrated how difficult Greene found it to set boundaries. He often stayed emotionally and financially attached to his former mistresses. When he left Dorothy Glover for Catherine Walston, he set up a pension for her and helped her buy a house in the country. After Dorothy's death, he arranged her funeral and provided for her aged mother. Yvonne noted in her memoir that Greene cried only twice in her presence; the first time was when Dorothy Glover died.

After his breakup with Catherine Walston, she continued to depend upon him as her health declined. During one of her convalescences, he traveled with her to Capri so that she could recover at the Villa Rosario. Yvonne was aware of this and accepted it as another of Graham Greene's eccentricities, like buying a house for Anita Björk, a Swedish actress he had been involved with before he committed to Yvonne. Love for Greene was never free. For all his efforts to remain footloose, he was as tied down as an uxorious husband.

HOPING TO UNSCRAMBLE my British publishing snafu, I hired a solicitor in London. I had signed a two-book contract with Jonathan Cape that called for them to publish *Life for Death* before bringing out my novel *Land Without Shadow*. But with *Life for Death* already in galleys, Cape shelved both titles pending a resolution of the libel case in the States. I protested that contractually they had no right to do this. Because they believed otherwise, I started paying legal bills in pounds sterling as well as in dollars.

Then a miracle occurred. Or as Greene had expressed it in *Brighton Rock*, "the appalling strangeness of the mercy of God" gathered me to its bosom. In London, I ran into a literary agent at a cocktail party the day John McEnroe beat Björn Borg in the 1981 Wimbledon final. Ignorant of the game, the agent was easily impressed by what he regarded as my expertise and bet that he could get me a contract to cover the men's tour and write a book about the experience. When I asked what I figured to make from the deal, he said twenty-five thousand pounds (about fifty thousand dollars).

"And what's in it for you?" I said.

"Ten percent."

That night I drew up a proposal. The agent read it and the next day told me to meet him at an Italian restaurant in

Soho for lunch. An editor from Collins joined us. He hadn't any idea that previously my largest advance in the United Kingdom amounted to a meager fifteen hundred pounds. He drafted a deal memo on a paper napkin, and that afternoon I relayed the news to Owen Laster, my U.S. agent, who quickly negotiated a matching fifty-thousand-dollar contract for the American rights.

Because Greene was bored to tears with tales from religious zealots about God's intervention in their lives, I deemphasized the divine when reporting these events to him. I described my new project as "something along the lines of Paul Theroux's *The Great Railway Bazaar* but with tennis, instead of trains, as the thematic frame." As things evolved, *Short Circuit* surprisingly became more like Greene's *The Lawless Roads*. Instead of an investigation of the persecution of Catholics in Mexico, my book exposed serious ethical and financial improprieties in pro tennis.

Setting out on the circuit, I had loved the sport and planned to produce a lyrical hymn to it. But I soon realized I had embarked on roads every bit as lawless as those Greene had traveled. At the first tournament, players, agents, umpires, and other stakeholders in the sport blithely discussed, in my presence, what the tennis press routinely concealed from fans. Before they agreed to play, the top-ranked stars demanded illegal bribes, or guarantees. Having paid out enormous sums of money, often more than a hundred thousand dollars before a single ball was struck, tournament directors took steps to protect their investment. They tinkered with the draw and arranged schedules to benefit guarantee-taking competitors. They pressured umpires to call close points in favor of the stars. Making a mockery of the Code of Conduct, officials turned a blind eye to match fixing, prize-money splitting, betting, and drug abuse.

To me, the most unnerving aspect of the corruption was its casualness. Nobody bothered to hide it. No Woodward or Bernstein was needed to dig up evidence. But the tricky part was calculating the risks of exposing the story. Leery of being sued again, this time by plaintiffs with very deep pockets, I insisted that my publishers indemnify me. Otherwise I would abandon the book. In the end, they agreed to include me under their insurance umbrella, and I followed the circuit as it snaked its way to Nice and Monte Carlo.

While in the South of France, I had hoped to spend a day with Graham Greene in Antibes. But he didn't answer his telephone or reply when I rang the intercom on Avenue Pasteur. At his age, close to eighty, all sorts of unpleasant scenarios seemed possible. But not the kind of trouble that had actually sent him into hiding.

As I gleaned first from newspaper reports, then from Greene himself when I finally spoke to him, he had accused Jacques Médecin, the mayor of Nice, of turning the Côte d'Azur into the Côte d'Ordure, the Garbage Coast. In homage to Émile Zola's famous defense of Alfred Dreyfus, Greene drew up a bill of particulars entitled *J'Accuse*, a bilingual pamphlet in French and English. He had a deeply personal stake in this case: Yvonne Cloetta's daughter, Martine, had become embroiled in a bitter divorce from her husband, Daniel Guy, whom Martine charged with verbal and physical abuse. Fighting for custody of their children and fearing that Guy might kill her, Martine convinced Greene that Guy had protectors in high places, perhaps even in Jacques Médecin's office.

It was only after their marriage that Martine had discovered that Guy had a criminal record and was still in touch with underworld cronies. Backed by crooked cops and compromised judges and politicians, Guy had gone so far as to assault Jacques Cloetta, Martine's father, whose complaints to the police prompted no action.

In an attempt to convince Guy to be reasonable and to abide by the terms of the divorce, Greene confronted the man, whose response was to brandish a fist in Greene's face. Fearing now for his own life, Greene began carrying a teargas canister.

Because there appeared to be no chance of a solution at the local level, Greene appealed to the Chancellor of the Legion of Honor and surrendered his lapel pin in protest. He copied his letter of resignation to Alain Peyrefitte, the Minister of Justice. Peyrefitte, an author himself, dispatched a team of detectives to Nice to investigate the situation.

Press coverage in France initially focused more on Graham Greene than on Daniel Guy or Jacques Médecin. Gossip circulated that he was involved because of his love affair with Martine's mother, Yvonne Cloetta. Greene attempted to laugh this off, observing that at his age he was flattered by the accusation. When questions about Yvonne persisted, he conceded that they had been intimate in the past, but maintained that that had nothing to do with the current miscarriage of justice.

The publication of *J'Accuse* ignited a barrage of suits and countersuits, and rigorous French laws against invasion of privacy and defamation transformed a banal civil case into a more serious matter. At a hastily called hearing, the court issued a decree that *J'Accuse* be withdrawn from sale and all remaining copies destroyed.

Still, seventeen thousand books sold, and Greene repeated the same charges in *Getting to Know the General*, his account of his friendship with Omar Torrijos. The dictator offered Martine and her children asylum in Panama. If she preferred to stay in Europe, he promised to furnish her with a new identity and a Panamanian passport. In his journal, Greene acknowledged that he and Torrijos and his bodyguard "spoke of killing" Daniel Guy. "I pretended that I would think it over," Greene hedged.

As Douglas Johnson remarked in the *London Review of Books*, *J'Accuse* appeared to be composed of bits and pieces drawn from Greene's vast bibliography. All the major themes of his fiction were present—marital friction, betrayal and deceit, petty criminality, political skullduggery, and violence. Cleverly splicing parenthetical quotes from Greene's novels into a synopsis of *J'Accuse*, Johnson concluded, "Doubtless all of [Greene's] actions, and this record of them, have been caused by his sympathy for poor Martine."

After his unhappy marriage and long string of failed love affairs, was Greene trying to prove to Yvonne and to himself that he was capable of loyalty? Or in light of his history as an indifferent father to his own children, was he attempting to demonstrate a paternal side? Of course it was possible *J'Accuse* was just another instance of Greene curing his depression with a good fight.

Whatever his motives, the results reiterated Somerset Maugham's astringent judgment that the Riviera was a sunny place for shady people. Jacques Médecin and his father had virtually owned the Nice mayor's office for over sixty years. After the uproar and investigation provoked by *J'Accuse*, Jacques Médecin fled to Uruguay. He was extradited to stand trial in France, then jailed for embezzlement and fraud.

This episode cost Greene a great deal of time, energy, and money, not to mention frequent whispers that he must have been going senile to get involved. Yet he continued to write—his new novel, *Monsignor Quixote*, came out in 1982— and continued to travel back and forth to Panama. Not even cancer of the colon could stop him. After he had part of his intestines surgically removed, he joked to me that he now had something in common with Ronald Reagan; they had had the same operation. But he promised that, unlike Lyndon Johnson, he wouldn't bare the fifteen-inch scar on his belly to the public.

That spring, I wrote to Greene:

> What an extraordinary, appalling and frightening business you've all been through. I hope [*J'Accuse*] has changed the situation for the better . . .
>
> "My own legal situation grinds on and on. It looks likely I'll have to stand trial for libel this fall in America. . . . There is now some talk that the plaintiff would be willing to accept an out-of-court settlement, which no doubt is what he wanted from the start. As awful as it would make me feel to give anything to the bastard, I may be forced to if I hope to go on and write something else.

After squandering twenty-five thousand dollars on lawyers' fees, I paid Lee Dresbach twenty-three thousand dollars to drop the suit without an admission of guilt on my part. The next time I saw Greene, he assured me I had been wise to settle. He had had some good news in his own case. Martine had won custody of her kids and relocated to Switzerland, beyond the grasp of her ex-husband and his low-life pals.

Greene announced that we should celebrate and led the way to Chez Félix au Port. Despite the happy face he put on for my benefit, he looked worn down and much older than the last time I saw him. His doleful eyes were deep socketed in wrinkled skin. His shoulders stooped more than ever. Tottering, he tilted forward as he walked. His frailty frightened me, and it hit me that he was an old man, not a monument. I wouldn't have him forever.

Yvonne was with us, disarticulating a fish with fine dexterity and apparently complete concentration. But she always absorbed more than anyone would have guessed, and she must have been as distressed as I was when he revealed that he had recently reached an agreement with his publisher. In response to gossip that he was losing his marbles, Greene said, "I told my editor to be ruthlessly honest. If I submit a book that sounds gaga, I want him to say so."

I made a dismissive gesture. But he insisted, "I'm serious. I've seen too many writers end up publishing drivel because no one had the courage to tell them the truth."

It's said of great athletes that they die twice—once when they retire from the limelight, then again when they draw their last breath. Something similar holds true for most authors. Usually they go deathly silent before they actually die. But figures of Greene's stature and sales record face a different dilemma. They can keep publishing long after they've lost the plot. With typical sangfroid, Greene was at pains to make sure that that fate didn't befall him.

A second revelation added weight to the notion that Greene recognized he was nearing the end. He had decided to sell his house on Capri, the place where he had worked well and enjoyed privacy with various lovers.

Greene astonished me by suggesting that I buy the Villa Rosario. Had our summers at Montclair led him to assume I was wealthy? Or was he convinced that after years in Rome I must have mastered *l'arte di arrangiarsi*—the art of fiddling things. In a roundabout fashion, he seemed to suggest there was something dodgy about his ownership of the villa. This was far from uncommon in southern Italy, where real estate deals are often shot through with murky property titles. Greene may have hesitated to sell the Villa Rosario on the open market for fear that someone would pop up with a prior claim on it.

Considering the implausible way Greene came into possession of the house, anything was conceivable. According to Michael Korda's memoir, *Charmed Lives: A Family Romance*, in the spring of 1948, Graham Greene and Michael's uncle, the legendary film producer Alexander Korda, were having difficulty with the script for *The Third Man*. Their brainstorming stuttered and stalled as they cruised along the Italian coast aboard Alexander Korda's luxurious yacht, *Elsewhere*, a converted torpedo boat, 120 feet in length. As an impressionable fifteen-year-old, Michael Korda was one passenger among a roster of celebrities; Randolph and Pamela Churchill, Vivien Leigh, and the director Carol Reed were on board. Taking the boy under his wing, Greene introduced him to dry martinis, a brothel in Nice, and a drag show in Genoa.

As Michael Korda remembered it, when they anchored off Capri, Greene gazed longingly at the island, saying, "I should give anything to own a villa there." The next morning, like a magus capable of granting all wishes, Alexander Korda tucked a rusty key into Greene's breakfast napkin. The previous night he had gone ashore and bought the villa Greene yearned for. "It's in your name, dear boy," Korda said. "Now the rest of my story, please." Whereupon the screenplay for *The Third Man* poured magically from Greene's imagination.

This was the kind of cute anecdote that Hollywood has always embraced. But beneath its gauzy surface, there was a pragmatic subtext that would have made sense to a sharp trader like Alexander Korda, deeply knowledgeable about fudging international currency regulations. Korda probably paid for the villa with money that was blocked in Italy. Then he signed it over to Greene in lieu of a salary, saving on taxes for both of them. Now, decades later, Greene, I speculated, needed to unload the villa without exposing its irregular provenance.

It didn't occur to me until later that Greene may have had alternative reasons for offering me the Villa Rosario at a discount. Perhaps he was paying forward the fantasy that Alexander Korda had fulfilled for him. Perhaps he was extending the same kindness he had lavished on friends and former mistresses to whom he had given financial support and, yes, houses. It wasn't out of character for him to help a writer, now nearly forty, who didn't appear likely to ever own a house. That I was in no position to take advantage of his generosity—the libel suit had wiped us out—doesn't diminish the magnanimity of the gesture.

Or am I simply piling fictional upon fictional possibility? The facts should be sufficient unto themselves. Greene's script of *The Third Man* got made and was a masterpiece. Greene received the Villa Rosario as payment and wrote other masterpieces there. When he eventually found a buyer for the house, he used the proceeds to purchase an apartment in Switzerland, where he went to die. As for my fantasy of owning a villa on Capri, that remains a Technicolor dream down to this day.

XIV

~~~~~~~~~~~~~

MY STEPFATHER, TOMMY Dunn, a heavy smoker and drinker since his teens, contracted lung cancer in 1982 and died at the age of sixty-seven. Mom swore he had been sober for the last year of his life and she thought we should thank God for taking him before he backslid into drunkenness. He and I had always had, at best, a fractious relationship. Tommy had never forgiven me for the time I shoved him to the floor.

He harbored another resentment that still resonates for me. In second grade, as I prepared to receive my First Communion, a nun urged members of the class to suggest that their parents receive the sacrament along with them. For me, this was out of the question. My mother and stepfather had divorced and remarried, which meant automatic excommunication. My childhood had been haunted by the conviction that my parents were going to hell.

Strictly forbidden to mention my mother's previous marriage, I felt I had already committed a sin when, under duress, I blabbed to the nun why my parents couldn't kneel next to me at the Communion rail. But Sister John Patrick spotted a loophole. If Mom and Tommy agreed to live together as brother and sister, they could return to the sacraments. This was known as a Josephite marriage, she explained.

Hurrying home to break the good news, I expected to be greeted with gratitude, not the tongue lashing I got from my mother and not the undying enmity of my stepfather. From then on, Tommy upbraided me for ruining his marriage and his life. In my teens, he spelled it out for me; after I suggested they live together as brother and sister, my mother refused to have sex with him. Though this wasn't the worst thing he ever said about her—he claimed she was working as a whore near a Navy base when he met her and he accused her of having a baby with a priest—it was his one wild accusation that I believed to be true. Ever since, I've been plagued with guilt about the harm I did him.

In October 1983, after a spell on the road promoting *Short Circuit*, I realized I hadn't spoken to Philip Mayer for months. Because he had introduced me to tennis, I thought he would appreciate my insight into the sad realities of the pro tour. I phoned him from Rome, and when Claire recognized my voice, she started to sob. "I should have told you. But I couldn't bring myself to call. Philip is dead."

I wish Claire, like my mother when she delivered bad news, had warned me to sit down. My knees buckled and I struggled to stay upright. He had died weeks ago, alone in a Dublin hotel, of a heart attack brought on by diabetes. "He wasn't careful about his health," Claire said. "He didn't follow a regimen like diabetics should. He didn't monitor his blood sugar and do his injections on schedule. He wouldn't stop risking his life."

She reminded me of his freelance reporting, his jaunts to Alabama and Mississippi to register Black voters, his trip to Prague during the 1968 Russian invasion, his stubbornly staying on in Phnom Penh as Pol Pot closed in on the city. When the Dublin hotel found his body, Claire said, they had no idea how to contact his family until they discovered a letter in his coat pocket from his daughter Kiki. From the return address they tracked Kiki down in San Francisco and informed her that her father was dead.

"Imagine her shock," Claire said. "Imagine my shock when Kiki called me. He was just 63 years old. Our first thought was to rush to him. He was so alone."

That's how I felt after I hung up—alone.

IN JULY 1985, Claire let us use her apartment in La Bocca, outside of Cannes, while she was away. Philip's library lined the walls of much smaller rooms now and the books reminded me of him and of our talks. For the first time I realized how reading links you not just to a writer. It can also create a connection with the person who introduced you to the book.

In a similar vein, I believed I'd always stay linked to Graham Greene. Reading his novels, reading the articles he wrote and the ones written about him, keeping current with the letters he shot off to newspapers, I had the sense that we were caught up in an ongoing conversation that continues to this day.

During our time in La Bocca, I braved the coast road to Antibes through torrents of summer traffic to join Greene and Yvonne at Chez Félix au Port. The city had sprouted up around the restaurant, everything larger, flashier, more upscale and expensive. A new pay parking lot glinted with polished cars between the town wall and the water. In the harbor, huge yachts dwarfed the old fishing boats.

Despite the crowds and cacophony, Greene was in high spirits and eager to discuss of all improbable subjects Aaron Burr, the U.S. vice president who, in 1804, shot and killed Alexander Hamilton. This scandalous duel had ended Burr's political career and rendered him a pariah for the rest of his life. Greene, who always sided with outcasts and sympathized with whoever appeared to be a victim—this could change, he admitted, in an instant—had read Gore Vidal's novel *Burr* and enjoyed it immensely. "I noticed on the flap copy that Vidal lives in Rome. Do you know him?"

I did. Gore Vidal, as I described him, was a kind of honorary customs inspector who validated the arrival and departure of every writer who passed through Rome. In his penthouse above Largo di Torre Argentina, he presided over a contemporary salon with a guest list that ranged from cardinals to rent boys, from diplomats to film dubbers, from Italian authors such as Italo Calvino and Luigi Barzini to American literary grandees such as William Styron, William Gaddis, and Tennessee Williams. "Vidal also has a villa in Ravello," I told Greene, "a great white stucco place plastered to a cliff like a bird's nest. I'm surprised your paths haven't crossed on the Amalfi Coast."

"I've never met him," Greene said, "but I should like to." This was the first and only time I ever heard him declare he wanted to meet someone.

"I have his address. Shall I tell him you'll be in touch?"

"Yes, please."

Thus began another of the odd pairings in Graham Greene's life. Although not as intriguing as his encounters with Ho Chi Minh or Fidel Castro or Omar Torrijos, the acquaintance between a guilt-ridden, obsessively heterosexual Roman Catholic and a guilt-free, gay libertine suggests how tolerant and eclectic both men were. They shared an affection for Italy, a thirst for alcohol, courageous positions on political controversies, and productivity that lasted late into their lives. After they participated on a 1987 panel in Moscow discussing nuclear arms reduction, Vidal told me how much he enjoyed drinking with Greene; Greene, in turn, told me that of all the people he met there, Vidal impressed him the most.

In second place, Greene said, was a Russian cosmonaut who claimed to have carried a copy of *Our Man in Havana* into space. Greene was repeatedly amused when his books surfaced in strange places—such as the opium den in Saigon where he spotted two of his novels next to the couch where he was smoking a pipe. On instinct he autographed the books.

WHEN JACQUES CLOETTA flew in from Africa for his annual reunion with his wife and family, Greene never said whether he resented these interruptions. My impression was that he appreciated the opportunity to travel. This year, he had scheduled a trip to London to screen a rough cut of the film of *Monsignor Quixote*. Then he would join Father Duran for a drive around Spain. Afterward, when he had Yvonne to himself, they planned to fly to Washington, D.C., where he would speak at Georgetown University, which had purchased some of his papers.

I encouraged him to make a side trip from D.C. to Charlottesville, where I was sure the University of Virginia would welcome him. I promised to get in touch with Douglas Day and have him set up something "easy and informal."

After so many frustrated attempts to entice Greene to Texas, I had little confidence he would make it to Georgetown, much less to UVA. But afterward he wrote to me that the rough cut of *Monsignor Quixote* in London had been "excellent," the trip to Spain "very tiring," and the excursion to the States a grand success:

> Yvonne and I both had a very good time in Washington. She had never been in America before and I had been twice in Washington, but this time we really saw the city which must be one of the three most beautiful capital cities in the world. We stayed in one of the best hotels I have encountered (if one ignores the food) the Madison, and Jo Jeffs, the [Georgetown] librarian, was the perfect host, guarding us as well as guiding us. My question and answer session went off very well—standing room only and very generous applause, but I was disappointed to have no political questions which would have enabled me to launch on the subject of Reagan's Central American policy. All I could do was get in a dig at the Pope.
>
> We passed one night at the execrable Hilton in Charlottesville and saw Douglas Day and enjoyed the visit very much—apart from the Hotel.

Greene's fussiness about food and hotels didn't surprise me. He was probably the only passenger in history to fly the Concorde and complain about the quality of the cheese.

The next time I saw him, he described a Black gay Catholic priest he had encountered in Charlottesville. The man impressed him by delivering a homily that was electrifyingly different from the usual droning sermons that parishioners doze through. Greene speculated that the priest might be an emblem of the modern Church—someone who had taken vows he couldn't possibly keep, preaching to a congregation that treated him as a pariah even though they depended on him. He was the reincarnation of the whisky priest in *The Power and the Glory*.

WITH EACH PASSING year, Linda and I mulled over—at times we argued over—whether to return to the States or remain in Italy. Friends and family and even casual acquaintances expressed bewilderment at our lives. A whiff of suspicion has long attached itself to U.S. citizens who resist living in the land of the brave and the home of the free. Aware that if I couldn't provide a good excuse, a bad one would be imputed to me, I cobbled together defenses against the kinds of accusations that Hemingway satirized nearly a century ago in *The Sun Also Rises*: "You're an expatriate. You've lost touch with the soil. You get precious. Fake European standards have ruined you. You drink yourself to death. You become obsessed with sex."

Out of orneriness, I never admitted to anything as insipid as being inspired by Italy. Nor did I protest that I sought refuge from American philistinism. I stressed to my consumer-minded fellow countrymen that staying abroad was a smart business proposition. Tongue tucked firmly in cheek, I spoke of the low cost of living in Italy and the terrific tax break. The IRS granted a seventy-five-thousand-dollar deduction to U.S. citizens who resided overseas.

When this didn't persuade people, I quoted Gore Vidal, who, when pressed to account for his forty-year exile in Italy, claimed he had modeled his behavior on Howard Hughes's. The multimillionaire had frittered away his youth as a swashbuckling aviator, a movie producer, the inventor of the uplift bra, and an avid bedder of beautiful starlets. Then mysteriously he retreated to a darkened hotel room, grew his hair down to his shoulders, let his fingernails and toenails turn into talons, and shuffled around in Kleenex boxes instead of shoes. When asked why he lived like that, Hughes, according to Vidal, said, "It's just something I drifted into."

This admission of drift generally got a laugh and got me off the hook. But questions I dodged in public still dogged me in private: Should we stay or go?

WHEN *THE CAPTAIN and the Enemy* came out, in 1988, I complimented Greene on what proved to be his last novel. I might have mentioned that the story reminded me of something written by his distant relative Robert Louis Stevenson. But I feared this would sound condescending.

A mysterious stranger wins a boy in a card game and leaves him with an equally strange female recluse who depends on the boy to update her with news of the outside world. Only at the end, in Panama, are identities revealed and the plot resolved. *The Captain and the Enemy* has the fablelike quality of a children's book—which isn't to say it was "childish." For all its simplicity, it's a sophisticated achievement that calls to mind Pablo Picasso's comment: "It took me four years to paint like Raphael, but a lifetime to paint like a child." In old age Greene was regaining a child's crystalline vision of the world.

A FAMOUS FELLOW British author, a Catholic no less, lived in Monaco, twenty miles from Greene's apartment. Anthony

Burgess and Graham Greene knew one another, yet seldom socialized. Still, Burgess remained a faithful acolyte to Greene's high priest. He applauded Greene's books in reviews and on TV talk shows and at literary festivals. Burgess dedicated his novel *Devil of a State* to Greene and delivered a radio lecture celebrating Greene's seventy-fifth birthday.

Legend has it that their relationship commenced when Greene contacted Burgess in Malaysia, where he then lived, and begged a favor. Greene had ordered some bespoke silk shirts and asked Burgess to deliver them to him in London. One version holds that opium had been sewed into the shirt cuffs and that Burgess knowingly smuggled dope to Greene. Another version claimed Burgess was kept in the dark and had no idea that he was carrying drugs—a capital offense in Malaysia.

Whichever tale is true, Burgess in a sense remained Greene's bag man. In 1973, he declared, "Let me say at once that *The Honorary Consul* is as fine a novel as [Greene] has ever written—concise, ironic, acutely observant of contemporary life, funny, shocking, above all compassionate." Yet this adulation prompted a tart letter from Greene. In a tone uncomfortably familiar to me, Greene challenged Burgess's journalistic accuracy. "Just to set the record straight about your very generous broadcast; it was not *The Heart of the Matter* which was condemned by the Holy Office, but *The Power and the Glory*, and it was *The Power and the Glory* that Pope Paul VI had read. It does make a good deal of difference because in my opinion *The Heart of the Matter* would quite rightly be condemned but not *The Power and the Glory*."

For all of Greene's nitpicking about the errors of other writers, he was prone to getting his own published facts wrong. With *An Impossible Woman*, the book about a colorful, obstreperous doctor on Capri, he was criticized by citizens of the island for committing obvious errors. His daughter, Lucy, had to correct the record when Greene wrote a mistaken description of the ranch in Canada he bought for her.

Eventually, Burgess came to resent what he viewed as Greene's ingratitude. While Greene had admired Burgess's early work, his enthusiasm turned lukewarm, then ice cold. Greene wrote to a friend, "I thought *Earthly Powers* was terrible. [Burgess] writes far too much. Apparently he was wildly indignant that he hadn't got the Nobel Prize instead of [William] Golding."

Greene told Gore Vidal that he found Burgess's boisterous self-promotion, particularly his appearances on TV talk shows, distasteful and contemptible. In view of Vidal's mantra that sex and television were opportunities a writer should never turn down, one wishes Vidal's reply had been recorded.

Hostilities between the two writers didn't break into the open until Burgess published an interview that Greene dismissed as absurd. Burgess's autobiography recounts his side of the controversy: "I went to Antibes to interview Graham Greene for the *Observer*. Greene's apartment was only a hundred yards up the hill from the Antibes station, but I had to take a taxi. Greene, in his middle seventies living with a chic French *bourgeoise* whose leg was not broken, was fitter than I at sixty-three. We talked and I bought him lunch . . . when I sent him the typescript of our colloquy [he] accepted that this was a true account. I did not of course use a tape recorder. Later, he contributed to 'Sayings of the Week' in the *Observer* the following remark: 'Burgess puts words in my mouth which I had to look up in the dictionary.' This turned me against him. He had long, it seemed, had something against me."

Burgess speculated that the style and substance of their books had put them at odds. "I had elected the Joycean way in the sense of deliberate hard words (to check the easy passage of the reader, in the manner of potholes on the road) and occasional ambiguity. Greene had made the popular novel of adventure his model. But I felt that the real barrier between us was that between the cradle Catholic and the convert."

This threw down the gauntlet for a dispute that continued until Greene's death. In 1988, speaking to the French magazine *Lire*, Burgess described Greene as an old man of eighty-six who had no friends and who isolated himself in Antibes corresponding on a daily basis with Kim Philby in Moscow. Reiterating his remark about the difference between cradle Catholics and converts, Burgess leveled the charge that Greene was guilty of class prejudices and had never embraced the whole Church body, which in England was dominated by the Irish, along with social outcasts like the Italians.

This was a criticism that had nettled Greene off and on throughout his career. Forty years earlier, George Orwell had accused *The Heart of the Matter* of theological snobbery and wisecracked that in Greene's novels, "Hell is a sort of high class night club, entry to which is reserved for Catholics only . . . He yearns to share the idea, which has been floating around since Baudelaire, that there is something rather *distingué* in being damned."

While Orwell appears to have gotten away with his wisecrack, Greene fired back at Burgess: "I know how difficult it is to avoid inaccuracies when one becomes involved in journalism, but as you thought it relevant to attack me because of my age (I don't see the point) you should have checked your facts. I happen to be 83, not 86, and I hope you will safely reach that age."

"In *Lire* you seemed to be quoted as writing that I had been in almost daily correspondence with Kim Philby before his death . . . In fact I received ten letters from him in the course of twenty years . . . Were you misinformed or have you caught the common disease in journalism of dramatizing at the cost of truth?"

Later that day, June 19, 1988, Greene's rage hadn't abated: "I have now received another cutting in which you claim I told you of an aggrieved husband shouting through my window (difficult as I live on the fourth floor). You are either a liar or you are unbalanced and should see a doctor. I prefer to think that."

The next time I visited, in the summer of 1988, Greene was still stewing about Burgess. His fingers, especially those stiffened by Dupuytren's contracture, trembled, and his pale complexion was aflame with broken veins. I hated seeing Greene in this state. It reminded me of my mother at her lowest moments, when I often played court jester to humor her out of bad moods. This was the role I had now fallen into with Greene.

"Burgess is a fool," I told him.

"Do you know him?"

"Let me tell you what happened when we met and you'll never take the man seriously again."

As usual, we were at Chez Félix au Port. Yvonne wasn't with us. But Sandy perched on the chair between Greene and me and appeared to follow the narrative, pivoting its head back and forth.

In Rome in 1971, I told him, I received a letter from Anthony Burgess forwarded by my publisher. Burgess had read the galleys of *Waking Slow* and responded with an enthusiastic blurb. "A poignant piece of invention . . . It's essentially a true picture of America today, and its talent is very formidable. Such solid construction, such fluency, such totally credible characterization make this a very memorable novel."

"He's thoroughly promiscuous with his blurbs," Greene broke in.

"I agree. But his address and phone number in Rome were on his letter. He lived a few blocks from Linda and me. So I decided to thank him in person."

At this remove in time it's difficult to recall the multifaceted role Anthony Burgess played in the seventies and eighties cultural life on both sides of the Atlantic. Almost as peripatetic as Greene, he had boomeranged around the globe. Before settling in Monte Carlo, he touched down in the Far East, on the island of Malta, at various American colleges, and in Italy. This hectic migration, always a step ahead of the tax authorities, never slowed his production of novels, biographies, criticism, filmscripts, plays, and librettos. A phenomenon as indefatigable as the weather, he published more than fifty books in the course of a career that was kick-started, according to legend, by a doctor's dire prediction that he was dying of a brain tumor. To create a financial cushion for his wife's imminent widowhood, he churned out four novels in a year.

"I question the truth of that legend," Greene interrupted again. "I wrote *The Lawless Roads* and *The Confidential Agent* in 1939, when I was also working on *The Power and the Glory*. That almost killed me. I couldn't have done it without drugs."

He had described this harrowing period in *Ways of Escape*: "Six weeks of a Benzedrine breakfast diet left my nerves in shreds and my wife suffered as the result. At five o'clock I would return home with a shaking hand, a depression which fell with the regularity of a tropical rain, ready to find offense in anything, and to give offense for no cause. For long after the six weeks were over, I had to continue with smaller and smaller doses to break the habit. The career of writing has its own curious forms of hell."

"Maybe," I said, "Burgess followed your Benzedrine diet."

In addition to producing books, Burgess played the piano and sang, wrote musical scores, and boasted of mastering a dozen languages. He characterized his best-known novel, *A Clockwork Orange*, as a philosophical treatise on free will, as well as a Russian lesson. Its cast of juvenile delinquents spoke an argot that Burgess swore would teach readers several hundred words of Russian. Displaying a dazzling range of talents, he also adapted the Bible for a TV miniseries, *The Life of Jesus Christ*, and translated Giacomo Belli's poetry, rendering the spectacularly obscene Italian dialect into English that would shame a rap singer.

With so many more profitable ways to occupy himself, Burgess hardly seemed the sort to bother blurbing books. But as young novelists charged out of the blocks, Burgess read them all and said something kind about each one. Some cynics groused that he was promoting himself by attaching his name like a franchise label to every new book. Although it was dubious whether his endorsement sold many copies, an author who didn't get a quote from Anthony Burgess might fear that he was starting off with a strike against him.

So I was relieved that he deigned to put his imprimatur on my second novel. When I called Burgess to thank him, his wife answered the phone. Not the wife whose widowhood he had hastened to provide for. That wife had died soon after Burgess's demise had been wrongly forecast. He had taken up with an Italian named Liana.

"Are you a friend to Anthony?" She pronounced it *Antony*. "Can you come here quick? Some badness has happened and I need help."

"I'm not a friend," I told her. "Mr. Burgess wrote a blurb for my new novel and I wanted to thank him."

"If he read your book, you must be friends." Her voice throbbed with urgency, but I had lived long enough in Rome to know that many Italians have a histrionic manner that charges even commonplace exchanges with melodrama. "Please, please hurry."

"I don't want to interrupt Mr. Burgess's work," I said.

"Antony is not here. He is in Mini-soda, in Mini-apples making an opera. I have been *scipatta*," Liana said. "Two boys on a motorbike stole my handbag. I lost my money, my cards, my keys, everything! I am obliged to change the locks on the apartment, but I have a baby I can't leave alone. Robbers might break in while I am gone. *Per piacere*, help me."

Why she couldn't summon a locksmith to her apartment or park the baby with a neighbor, Liana didn't say and I didn't ask. Together Linda and I rushed across the Tiber to Trastevere. Then, as today, guidebooks referred to the area as a worker's quarter, a *rione* where authentic Romans live. But rows of boutiques had popped up like toadstools, selling scented candles, potpourri, and pirated cassettes.

The Burgesses' apartment, located on Piazza di Santa Cecilia, occupied the ground floor of a restored palazzo. In the front hall stood what I at first took to be a marble bust of a Roman emperor. On closer inspection, it proved to be a bust of Anthony Burgess, his Hibernian head crowned by curls as artfully sculpted as acanthus leaves.

Greene laughed out loud. "Burgess's hair never looks right

no matter whether he combs it over his bald spot or wears it flopping in his face."

Liana, by contrast, was perfectly coiffed. Short and shapely in hip-hugging slacks and knee-high boots, she introduced us to the "baby," a boy of six or seven named Andrea. Unlike his mother, who spoke English with a Sicilian accent, or his father, who had the posh pronunciation of a BBC newsreader, Andrea sounded like a Cockney street urchin.

Liana promised she wouldn't be gone long. "Just until I find a locksmith. There is food to eat, mineral water for drinking. Andrea is sometimes hungry." She paused at the door and drew a deep breath. "This all makes me so fastidious."

"Fastidious?" I looked blankly at Linda.

"She means bothered, flustered."

In his mother's absence, Andrea clambered around the kitchen, crawling up on the table, jumping off chairs. Back before we had children, other people's kids all seemed hyperactive and half-feral. Andrea finished monkeying around, then declared, "I'm bored."

So was I. An hour passed. Then another. Liana could have had the whole door replaced by now. Andrea said he was hungry, and Linda asked what he'd like to eat. The little guy canted his head and leered. "How about your bum?"

"That's not nice," I said.

"Have you tried it?" he taunted me.

Greene's laughter sent Sandy into a frenzy of barking. "The boy must have been quoting his father's dialogue."

When Andrea went into his bedroom, I hoped he meant to take a nap. But he bounded back dressed in a martial arts tunic. Flailing his tiny fists, kicking his feet, he struck a pose, left arm extended, right arm coiled. "It's time for karate."

I feared he meant to use us as punching bags. "Why don't you practice in your room?" I suggested.

"The *palestra* is just across the piazza."

"Your mother will take you when she gets back. She'll be here in a few minutes." Linda expressed my own fervent wish.

"You're going to make me miss it," Andrea squawked. "The maestro will be mad."

"Take him," I told Linda. "I'll stay and wait for his mother."

"What if she doesn't show up? That's what worries me," Linda said. "You don't suppose this is what it's like to have kids, do you?"

"Of course not."

"You were right to worry about children," Greene interjected. "They're as bad for a writer as Benzedrine."

"Liana was gone so long," I resumed, "I started to worry that she had had an accident. She could be in the hospital or dead. Without her handbag, she wouldn't have an identity card. The police wouldn't have a clue how to contact us. And how could we get in touch with Burgess in the States? If by some miracle we did locate him, who except Linda and me would look after Andrea until Burgess flew back from Mini-apples?

"By now it was late afternoon," I continued. "Linda and Andrea came back from karate practice. She looked frazzled and the boy was cranky and thirsty and demanded a glass of milk. Linda poured him one and he chugged it down and wiped his mouth on her sweater.

"When Liana finally breezed in, she offered no apology and no explanation, just more complaints about the sloth of Roman bureaucrats, the Byzantine closing hours. "It all makes me so fastidious," she moaned. "If you don't mind, I am too tired to entertain tonight. When Antony returns, we will invite you for dinner. Now I must rest and you must go."

"Go we did," I told Greene, "bolting for the door without a goodbye to Liana or a backward glance at Burgess's bust."

"So you didn't actually meet the man," Greene said. "Just his appalling wife and child."

"Wait. I'm getting to that."

The following spring, I had press credentials to the Cannes Film Festival, and among the new movies, none generated more controversy than Stanley Kubrick's production of *A Clockwork Orange*. Early reviews raved about Malcolm McDowell's performance as a classical music–loving sociopath and about the choreographed sexual assault scene. But then a second batch of articles attacked the film as anti-female, an incitement to violence, and exploitative of a fine novel for crude commercial purposes.

Burgess objected that his meditation on good and evil and free will had been trivialized. What's more, he felt ripped off, or so he said whenever he had a captive audience. Kubrick had bought the film rights at a bargain-basement price ages ago, when Burgess had been hard up for cash.

"He should have asked my advice," Greene said. "I would have warned him what Hollywood is like."

Piggybacking on the publicity blitz for the movie, Penguin hurried a paperback of *A Clockwork Orange* into print and arranged a series of interviews for the deeply affronted author. During the Cannes Film Festival, Burgess played no part in the official program, but he held a press conference at the Carlton Hotel. I attended, viewing this as a chance to thank him for his blurb and inquire whether new locks had been installed on his apartment.

The event attracted a hundred or so reporters and photographers. Unlike formal press conferences conducted in the Festival Hall, this one transpired amid a cluster of folding chairs in a Carlton conference room. Anthony Burgess arrived in a rumpled suit, with his hair laid across his forehead like a pair of lobster claws. Puffing a cigar, he delivered a lecture on the necessary correlation between free will and salvation. In an aside, he lampooned the multimillion-dollar screen version of his book and lamented that a fraction of its budget had not been spent publicizing his fiction.

As the floor opened for questions, there were professional translators on hand. But Burgess, the eminent polyglot, announced that their services wouldn't be needed except in the rare instance that a Magyar or Mayan wished to speak.

To everybody's shock, however, Burgess had trouble with French and did no better in Italian and Spanish. Not only did he misconstrue the questions; he flubbed his answers and couldn't string together coherent sentences. Perhaps he was nervous, perhaps hard of hearing, but as his famous fluency deserted him, the audience began to grumble.

A moderator suggested a translator might save time. Burgess was insulted and stuck to his garbled replies. When the moderator, without permission, imposed a translator, a woman in the audience leapt atop a chair and screamed, "Let him speak! Let him speak! Why must there be censorship?"

"Mike, you can't expect me to believe this," Greene protested, giggling and taking Sandy onto his lap to settle the dog down.

"I swear it's the truth."

While photographers snapped pictures, the woman pulled her dress up over her head. But not before I recognized Liana.

This persuaded Burgess to accept a translator, and once the press got the quotes it came for, the moderator said that copies of *A Clockwork Orange* were on sale; Mr. Burgess had graciously agreed to sign them.

I joined the line, I told Greene, and expressed my gratitude for Burgess's blurb. At the mention of my name, a dim flicker of recognition quickened his close-set eyes. "Why yes, what a pleasure to meet you." He pumped my hand. "Refresh my memory. Do I owe you something? A letter? A recommendation? Money?"

I swore the debt was all mine. Linda and I had spent a delightful day in Rome getting acquainted with his son Andrea.

"Yes, yes, Liana said you were a godsend. And your marvelous novel, is it doing well?" Burgess asked.

I confessed that three months after publication, it was on its way to the remainder table.

Anthony scowled. "Terrible business, publishing. I'd rather switch to writing librettos, that's the way to make money. Here, let me sign that."

On the inside cover of his novel, he scrawled his name, then sketched a hybrid orange that had numerals and bolts and springs exploding off a clock face. "After I tend to these other good people, Michael, why don't you and I have a drink on the terrace?"

I stepped aside. The next person in line clutched a reporter's spiral notepad. After chatting with Burgess for a minute or two, he moved over beside me. Plump and sun-pinkened, he wore white socks with open-toed sandals. "Are you a friend of Anthony's?" he asked.

"Just met him."

"He promised me an interview. He said you're a writer too and invited me to have a drink on the terrace with you."

I smiled. "Great."

"I'm glad you and Nigel have become friends," Anthony said once he finished autographing paperbacks. "Michael has just published a smashing novel," he told Nigel. "I expect he's in Cannes to explore the film possibilities. Your writing is so visual, Michael, your dialogue so spot on, they ought to let you have a crack at the script."

"Do you have a movie deal?" Nigel said, suddenly alert to new possibilities.

"A couple of lukewarm nibbles." This was a lie. To date, *Waking Slow* had prompted no film interest at all.

"Michael's novel is set in Los Angeles," Burgess said. "That automatically gives him a leg up. Some studio is sure to grab it."

Seated at a table far from the power spots overlooking La Croisette, the three of us must have seemed a sorry lot to the Carlton's haughty waiters. They hurricaned back and forth ignoring Nigel's *"Garçon!"* and Burgess's gesticulating cigar. Only after they had served the stars and the moguls did they get around to us. Since mixed drinks cost as much as I usually paid for a three-course meal, I ordered a *citron pressé*. Nigel and Anthony each had a glass of champagne. Burgess proposed a toast to literature.

"Actually," Nigel announced, "I'm more than just a journalist. I do a bit of creative stuff on the side."

"I had a hunch that might be the case." Burgess concentrated on the bubbles in his champagne.

"That's why it's such a thrill to meet you and get a chance to discuss ideas. And of course interview you."

"Queasy with recognition," I told Greene, "I realized what lay ahead and so did Burgess. Had I ever sounded as smarmy and Uriah Heepish as Nigel inching up on the big question—will you read my work?"

Burgess asked the waiter for a refill and said, "If you gentlemen will excuse me, I have to find a loo."

Reality didn't register at first on Nigel. He had faith Burgess would return. I knew better. I had read Burgess's *Enderby* novels, about a besieged poet who habitually hides in the bathroom. We could tarry here until nightfall. We could cool our heels until closing time and Anthony would never come back. Nigel's was one novel the Blurb King wouldn't be praising.

Normally I might have resented getting stuck with Nigel and stiffed for the drinks—one of which, Burgess's second champagne, was untouched. Instead, I admired the deftness with which he had shrugged the burden from his shoulders. Like a Zen master, he had absorbed our energy and flipped it against us.

I suggested that Nigel finish off Anthony's bubbly before it lost its effervescence. He didn't protest. By now he had guessed the score. I picked up the bill, wished Nigel the best of luck, and hurried off in a direction where I wasn't likely to bump into Burgess.

"WELL DONE," GREENE said. "Your best story since the banana burglar broke into your house. It'd be an awful shame if you didn't write it up."

Making him laugh pleased me as much as anything he had ever said in praise of my work. If I had realized then that this was the last time I would see Greene alive, his words would have meant even more to me. I would have said—What? That I appreciated all the kindness he had shown me over the years? That I would promise to honor his suggestion and turn the encounter with Anthony Burgess into an autobiographical essay?

XV

"**N**O HUMAN HEART changes half as fast as the face of a city," Charles Baudelaire said of Paris in the nineteenth century. Lord knows what he would have made of twentieth-century Rome, whose face never seemed to change, while its heart was as *mobile*, as fickle, as the Mediterranean weather.

My romance with Rome, ardent and erotic as it was at the start, had never been a placid marriage. More like a passionate love affair full of histrionic highs and bitter lows, it was punctuated by angry outbursts and fevered reconciliations. If, as the *New York Times* book critic Anatole Broyard once told me, I lived in Italy in an effort to resolve one form of alienation with another, the treatment no longer felt effective. The idiosyncrasies of the city that used to amuse me had started to rankle.

Still we stayed on, and ironically part of the reason we did so was the same one that prompted us to consider leaving. It came down to a question of the kids. Originally we believed that Europe was a treasure of inestimable value that we were bestowing on them. Then gradually we began to wonder whether we were doing Sean and Marc a disservice. Although Linda and I were confident we could reintegrate into the United States, we feared Sean and Marc might wind up marooned on a treacherous middle ground, neither wholly American nor entirely Italian.

When I sought advice from friends in the United States, they exclaimed, "Why would you ever leave Rome? Do you realize what it's like to raise kids here?" On the fingers of both hands, they counted off what they perceived as the advantages of an expat childhood. Our boys attended bilingual international schools whose student bodies were drawn from all races, creeds, and colors. Christians, Jews, Moslems, Hindi, Buddhists, and animists mixed on amiable terms. Cultural differences were occasions for discussion, not discord. History and art surrounded them in the street; field trips took them to the Wonders of the World. "Think of the essays they'll write for their college applications," friends raved.

Still, I regretted that Sean and Marc remained ignorant of the myriad shards that comprised the national mosaic of America. The World Series and the Super Bowl had meant less to them than Christians versus lions at the Colosseum. If we moved back, they'd spend years catching up on the names of teams and star players, pop singers, and TV shows. They wouldn't just feel like foreigners in their homeland. They'd be as befuddled as the tourists who bumbled through Rome, perplexed by the rate of exchange, confused by pay phones, hesitant to speak Italian for fear of spouting nonsense.

There was so much basic information the boys needed to absorb—granular tidbits that natives took for granted. One summer while visiting his maternal grandparents, Marc pressed a button on the bathroom wall. That's how you flushed the toilet in our Roman apartment. But things functioned differently in Pittsburgh, Pennsylvania, and Marc discovered to his astonishment that he had sounded an emergency alarm that summoned the police, who declined to stand down until they had searched the house. In a sense, that clamorous alarm continued to ring the whole time Linda and I debated whether to stay or leave.

At last I sent a letter to Greene announcing that Linda and I had stopped dithering:

> After years of discussion and debate we've moved back to the States," I wrote. "The transition has been eased by the University of Virginia and Douglas Day (whom you met here). I've been asked to be Visiting Writer. William Faulkner filled the same role just after he won the Nobel Prize, but somehow I don't think the pattern will hold in my case.
>
> I've just finished Norman Sherry's biography [volume I] and I found it a moving and, in many ways, a disturbing experience. Naturally I knew some of the information from your own books and from articles. But I suppose I never focused on how much trouble and turmoil you encountered early in your career. Seen from the outside, your life, especially after you started publishing, might seem to be one of serene success, triumph following triumph. So it is salutary to be reminded of the reality, the rough and tumble, that marks most writers' lives.

Greene replied:

> I am delighted to hear about the job at the University of Virginia. Personally I would find it impossible to make my

life in Italy. I am sure Virginia must be far more pleasant.

Personally I found Sherry's book far, far too long and I had difficulty in getting through it. The thought of another volume makes me shudder. I was surprised that on the whole it got such good reviews. The detective work was interesting but sometimes went astray.

By telephone Greene clarified his displeasure over Sherry's book. It embarrassed him to be confronted by the many saccharine love letters he had written Vivien during their courtship. Why not quote a couple of them and let it go at that? he wondered.

To add to Greene's consternation, Sherry had included cringe-worthy letters he had written to Dorothy Glover and to Catherine Walston while still having flings with prostitutes. Sherry didn't pass judgment on Greene's behavior; he let the reader draw his own conclusions.

Sherry did the same when exploring—or failing to explore—Greene's emotional problems. He noted Greene's numerous breakdowns, his bouts of therapy, his begging for electric shock treatment, his compulsive promiscuity, and his drinking and drug use—all without much authorial comment. At times it sounded as if Sherry were simply compiling lists—like Hemingway's biographers counting the kudus Papa shot and the sailfish he landed.

For decades, Greene had had sessions with Dr. Eric Strauss. While privacy rules denied Sherry access to Strauss's raw files, he could have dug deeper and consulted experts on bipolar pathology, placing Greene in the pantheon of authors who presented cases similar to his own. Kenneth Lynn's biography of Ernest Hemingway and Kay Redfield Jamison's book about Robert Lowell serve as examples of life stories that combine sympathy for the patient with astute clinical analysis of the individual's illness.

In 2020, Richard Greene's [no kin] biography, *The Unquiet Englishman*, did quote Dr. Jamison to the effect that it was "a triumph" that Greene didn't commit suicide. Otherwise, he stuck to "the story of Graham Greene's life and times," leaving his psychosexual history underexplored.

Ironically, a much-maligned biography by Michael Sheldon, *The Enemy Within*, contains some fascinating material about Greene's emotional makeup. While Sheldon's speculations about Greene's possible homosexuality and sadism seem dubious and at times distasteful, he reveals that Greene had an imaginary friend, Hillary Trench, whom he blamed for his bad behavior. Sheldon also claims that Greene packed a teddy bear as a good luck charm whenever he traveled; he was carrying it the day he was pinned down by gunfire on the Suez Canal. Sheldon's research also uncovered information that Kenneth Richard, the man Greene lived with in London as a teenager, supposedly for psychological support, had no medical degree and no training as a therapist.

"Greene's travel to remote areas of the world," Sheldon concluded, "were never as meaningful as his ongoing exploration of the more obscure places in the human imagination. [They were] his longest journey without maps."

Long before I met Greene, I imagined I understood him and I imagined that as he aged and his fame increased his suffering would diminish. I hoped that if that happened to him, it might happen to me. By building a wall of books around myself, I hoped to brick up the empty spaces inside me. Instead I learned, as Greene had, that "[f]or a writer and similarly for a priest there is no such thing as success."

Despite the jauntiness of my letters to Greene, I started to spiral into a very dark place. At first I assumed it was reverse culture shock, a failure to reacclimate to America in general and Charlottesville in particular. I missed Italy and diagnosed myself as Rome-sick.

The return to teaching contributed to my dismay. Other professors maintained that they found students a source of joy, even inspiration. They happily held classes in the evening at their homes and laid on hors d'oeuvres and drinks. I preferred to meet in a seminar room; half the reason I taught was to get out of my head by getting out of the house.

This disappointed my students, who soon soured on me. Or maybe I was the sour one. I wanted to help them become writers—even as I became increasingly disenchanted with the profession. Their stories struck me as hopeless, but then so did my own fiction.

My opinion shouldn't be taken as gospel on any of this. I may well have misread their work, just as I misread my mood. By the start of the second semester, I realized I wasn't Rome-sick. I was brain-sick, chemically out of whack, clinically depressed. This was a subject I might profitably have discussed with Graham Greene, who had survived many a plunge into sadness. Instead I peppered him with letters that sounded as if he, not I, needed cheering up:

> I write both to wish you a happy birthday—if memory serves it's coming up soon—and to let you have our new address. We're still in [Charlottesville], but have moved a

few miles away to another house belonging to a professor on leave.

We spent the summer in Rome where one of my novels (*Year of the Gun*), about the Red Brigades and Aldo Moro, is being made into a movie. I was supposed to be a 'consultant'—which was really a runner-up prize because I was never allowed to do any of the dozen or so scripts based on my book. Mostly I stayed in the hotel, wrote, and read your collection of letters to various newspapers. I enjoyed the letters enormously and was once again impressed by the range of your interests and the wickedness of your sense of humor.

Year of the Gun would prove to be the biggest payday of my career. The film generated more money than the advances of all my novels combined. Paperbacks with Sharon Stone plastered on the cover were reissued in France, Spain, Germany, and Italy. Hired as a consultant, I was flown first class to and from Rome and paid three thousand dollars a week essentially for playing tennis with the director, John Frankenheimer. At the age of forty-eight, after eight books and hundreds of articles and reviews, I had at last gained a measure of financial security and I felt . . .

I felt nothing. No joy, no pride, no satisfaction, not even a smidgen of relief. When the movie appeared and the producers asked me to fly to New York to participate in a panel discussion with John Frankenheimer at Columbia University, I refused. This became my fallback response to almost every request. Like Bartleby the scrivener, I preferred not to. Instead I seethed with anger that if *Year of the* Gun had been filmed a year earlier, I wouldn't have left Rome. I could have bought Graham Greene's house on Capri or Philip Mayer's villa in Auribeau.

When depressed, my mother moaned that she felt rats gnawing at her guts. Other times she said it was as if her throat had been slit—which frightened me as a kid because she actually had a wicked scar on her neck, the result of a thyroid operation. My own symptoms included bone-deep pain, never-ending nausea, and a dizzying drone in my head. It occurred to me that if my few years of depression were anything like Greene's lifelong suffering, I stood in awe of his endurance.

In the midst of my misery, in October 1990, news from Greene deepened my sadness. "I have not been at all well," he wrote, "and live between blood transfusions so that I am unable to travel farther than Switzerland. However we have got a beautiful new flat in Switzerland where we hope to spend a great deal of our time because it is so much quieter than Antibes and more beautiful."

Word leaked on the literary grapevine that Greene was suffering from leukemia. Yvonne denied this and insisted it was a different blood ailment, which she didn't name. In Corsair, Switzerland, there was a medical clinic close by, and his daughter and grandchildren, as well as Yvonne's, had relocated to the area. His apartment offered views of Lake Geneva and the Alps and the ruins of the Castle of Chillon. He asked that books from his Paris flat be shipped to him so that as his health failed, he was surrounded by familiar titles as if by old friends. He chose to read the collected letters of Ezra Pound, the disgraced antisemitic poet who had escaped imprisonment as a traitor and spent a dozen years confined to St. Elizabeth's mental hospital in Washington, D.C. Pound's pariah status probably appealed to Greene, as did the poet's belief that the best literature is news that stays new.

For much of Greene's life, he had struggled to evade all restraints, and the wide world, especially its most deprived and dangerous places, became his province. Wherever human lives, religious belief, or political freedom was at risk, Greene had traveled there to record the plight of the victims and reckon the body count.

Dying in Switzerland, not unlike living in Switzerland, had about it a banal domesticity that Greene had scorned. He had expected to be killed—at times he yearned for death—in Vietnam or Malaysia or in Kenya during the Mau Mau uprising. It was wildly out of character for him to die in a spanking-clean condo.

The first evening we met in Antibes he had disparaged Jacques Cloetta's Swiss citizenship as if to suggest he deserved to be cuckolded. Greene's script for *The Third Man* contains one of the most memorable monologues in cinematic history. Orson Welles, in the character of Harry Lime, quips, "In Switzerland, they had brotherly love, they had five hundred years of democracy and peace—and what did that produce? The cuckoo clock."

Although movie historians maintain that Welles ad-libbed these lines, they don't contradict Greene's sentiments. Yet here he was at rest, if not at peace, in a country he had reviled, his existence reduced, as he said, to going from room to room, transfusion to transfusion.

Yvonne remained faithfully at his side, offering sympathy and support. But Greene wasn't altogether receptive. According to Yvonne, he pushed her away and his last words were "But I want to go."

IN CHARLOTTESVILLE, MY life also seemed at a dead end. A stroll around town required more stamina, more willpower, than the overland trip from Samarkand to Bukhara I took for the *New York Times*. Mired in irascibility and irrationality, I managed to alienate everyone in the UVA English Department, including Douglas Day, my friend for thirty years. Had I recognized that Day was swan-diving into the same deep pool of dejection that was drowning me, we might have made common cause and helped save one another.

Among his papers, Day left a *cri de coeur* that he had written years earlier. "My God, one cries out in great fear—this must be put back, this must be fought off. I am sane, I am strong; I am only unhappy. Many have gone through worse. *Durchhalten*; hold fast; courage is all. Sit still, take a deep breath; choke it off; think of something else. . . . How many nights like this will there be before the awful conviction engulfs me, and I kill myself?"

While Douglas Day ended up committing suicide, I ended up, through sheer luck and certainly no virtue of my own, in therapy and on antidepressants. When he heard I had been prescribed Prozac, Pat Conroy, a friend, razzed me that I'd spend the rest of my life writing Hallmark greeting cards. Pat was wrong. I wrote books, but for ten years none of these found its way into print. I also wrote travel articles, reviews, and tennis coverage, which got me out of my head and out of the house.

I wonder whether a selective serotonin reuptake inhibitor might have changed Graham Greene's life and the course of twentieth-century literature. But I doubt he could have been persuaded to depend on pills. He had diagnosed his condition to his wife the day they separated: ". . . my restlessness, moods, melancholia, even my outside relationships [a euphemistic reference to his sexual adventures] are symptoms of a disease . . . Unfortunately, the disease is also one's material. Cure the disease [and] I doubt a writer would remain."

Even if it meant undermining myself as a writer, I preferred to try to cure the disease. I never mentioned this to Greene. Although I was well aware of his often expressed wish for death—his novels and nonfiction were saturated with it—he knew nothing about my emotional life. I can't accuse him of indifference. How could he know anything was wrong with me? Until the end, I stuck to my role as wisecracking court jester and attempted to give Greene a laugh whenever I could. Five days before he died, I sent what would be my last letter to him:

> I thought you might be amused by the enclosed clipping from the Washington Post. I know you have been bedeviled in the past by doppelgängers and imposters, but this carries things a step further. It seems there is now an American Graham Greene, an actor who has just been nominated for an Academy Award [for his supporting role in *Dances with Wolves*]. To top everything, he's an American Indian, an immense, long-haired man whose face might have been chiseled from stone. Do you suppose it's just a stage name? Or were his parents librarians or literature teachers on the Sioux reservation?
>
> We're more or less fine . . . the movie of *Year of the Gun* is scheduled for August, and I tremble to think of seeing it. I fear it'll be more ridiculous than most Hollywood movies. Apparently they re-created Aldo Moro's kidnapping in a small hill town. They told me Rome and

the intersection where the events actually transpired just wasn't picturesque enough.

Hope you are well, and that spring has reached Europe. Are you still in Switzerland? I'll send this to Antibes and hope it reaches you. Linda joins in sending warmest regards to you both.

GRAHAM GREENE DIED on April 3, 1991. Obituaries dominated newspapers around the world, and there were eulogies in literary journals, on radio, and on television. Even Anthony Burgess cobbled together a personal reminiscence less cantankerous than one might have predicted.

At first I felt nothing at the news of Graham Greene's death. It was like the day in Paris when my fist shattered a Metro window, slicing open my wrist. A heartbeat or two had to pulse by before my insulted nervous system processed the damage. Only as torrents of blood spouted from the gash had waves of pain poured through me and I understood what I had done to myself.

That's how Greene's death hit me—as something I had foolishly inflicted on us both. I thought, if only I had been more attentive . . . then what? Nothing in my power could have prevented his dying.

Among the things I regretted was that my most concerted effort to make explicit what he meant to me—my errant profile of him—had caused so much pain. And there were so many questions I hadn't asked and couldn't count on scholars to answer. So many subjects I had shied away from. Because we were both Catholic, people assumed that we had shared our sentiments about religion, comparing our doubts and beliefs. But our talks had rarely touched on these subjects.

His faith—how he felt about it, how he did or didn't practice it—seemed to me a deeply private matter. I wouldn't have challenged him any more than I would have quizzed him about his sex life.

More than most men Greene carried to the grave a heavy freight of secrets. A letter from Norman Sherry lay on his night table, pressing him again for information about his career as a spy and his connection with Kim Philby. Father Duran, who heard his last confession, said Greene was troubled until the very end by his involvement in British intelligence. Did he feel the need for forgiveness? Or simply understanding?

It grieved me that Greene and I had no friends in common, no one I could commiserate with, no one to sympathize with my sense of loss. I had never met a member of his family, and I knew no address where I might send condolences to Yvonne Cloetta. I had only one photo of the two of us, standing side by side in front of the sun-drenched Antibes harbor. And I had just one souvenir of our friendship—the signed mockup of a never published edition of *The Quiet American* more than half a century old. I feared I had been cut off forever.

But then one of the familiar blue envelopes landed in my mailbox. For a delirious instant, I fantasized that he was still alive, faithfully answering his correspondence. After reality reasserted itself, I hoped that he had had time to reply to my final letter. There flashed through my mind the scene from *The Heart of the Matter* when Major Scobie receives in reverse order two telegrams—the first announcing that his daughter "Catherine died this afternoon." Then the second: "Catherine seriously ill. Doctor has hope."

The envelope in my mailbox was from Amanda Saunders, Greene's niece:

Your letter to Graham Greene was forwarded to me from Antibes.

I was in Switzerland when Graham died and his last days were peaceful and painless. As you know he had been ill for some time and in the end he was very fed up with the way he was having to live his life. He was a great writer and also a great and generous spirit with a deep respect for all men. An enormous loss for all of us who loved and treasured him and we will miss him terribly.

In *The Heart of the Matter*, when Scobie mistakenly thinks there is hope for his daughter, he is seized by anxiety. But after he learns the truth, "then it was all right, she was dead. I could begin to forget her." My reaction to Greene's death wasn't at all like that. I couldn't forget him. I remembered him, his books, the days we spent together, the correspondence we exchanged over twenty years. He invaded my dreams.

In one of the most touching postmortems, Martin Amis recalled an interview with Greene in Paris on his eightieth birthday: "Graham Greene was inevitably the first serious writer you came across: he seemed exemplary adult and exemplary modern. Now he seems neither. Now he seems adolescent, though in the realist and (again) most romantic sense. It is a commonplace that his novels, for all their geographical variety, did not 'develop.' Greeneland stays the same . . . Graham Greene's influence none-the-less will remain deep and formative . . . He was an awakener."

I agree with Amis that Greene was an awakener whose influence remains deep and formative. I even agree that Greeneland has stayed the same. But I don't view that as a failure on

Greene's part. The sad truth is that vast stretches of the world haven't changed because the political and social suffering of people hasn't changed.

In *Greene on Capri*, Shirley Hazzard evoked, yet never romanticized, the times they shared on the island. The stated goal of her memoir was to recall what it was like "to walk with him in a street, to exchange opinions, literature, laughter, and something of one's self; to observe his moods and responses, suffer his temper, and witness his attachments: to see him grow old."

All of this, and more, she admirably accomplished. I've tried to do the same, but inevitably from a different perspective. Because of our Catholicism, our similar emotional baggage, our combative natures and obsession with travel, I believe it's likely that Greene and I knew one another in ways Hazzard couldn't. Then, too, her recollection of their relationship is one-sided. The reader never learns, because Hazzard never did, what Greene thought of her. But what Greene thought of me comes across in his letters, the bad along with the good.

In the end, Shirley Hazzard observed, "When friends die, one's credentials change; one becomes a survivor." And as a surviving friend I've felt it crucial to keep my credentials up to date—by remembering Greene and writing about him, by rereading his work and reviewing what others have written about him.

I have also continued to travel, going farther afield, just as he did, as I approach eighty. Some of these trips were linked directly to Greene, as when the *New York Times* dispatched me to Vienna to trace the plot of *The Third Man* through the city and its underground sewers. I've made it a point to spend time in places that mattered to Greene—Prague, Krakow, Moscow.

Then I drifted farther east into Central Asia on the Silk Road and eventually visited Laos, Cambodia, and Thailand. I spent a month in South Africa, and like Greene wound up in the hospital there. To celebrate my sixty-fifth birthday, traveling alone overland for three months without a camera or a phone or anything that would betray me as a tourist, I went from Alexandria, Egypt, to Tangier, Morocco, through Libya and Algeria, which are as deep into Greeneland as one can get and hope to survive.

To claim that I did this in emulation of Graham Greene or in admiration of him, much less in an effort to become him, isn't strictly true. Scholars and biographers may have followed in his footsteps in an attempt to understand him. I did so more in the determination to understand myself, to *be* myself. Being Graham Greene, as rich a prize as that had once seemed to me, entails a cost too great to be borne by anybody except the man himself. For all his frailty, he had incomparable courage and strength. Despite his occasional querulousness and quickness to anger, he had a forgiving soul. Whether he finally received forgiveness himself, God alone knows. Although he was often despondent, I like to remember him laughing, as he was that last day at Chez Félix au Port.

ACKNOWLEDGMENTS

Great thanks to my agent of more than forty years, Michael Carlisle; Joshua Bodwell, my patient editor; my sons Sean and Marc; the Graham Greene estate for permission to quote from his letters; Boston College and the Humanities Research Center at the University of Texas Austin for copies of my correspondence with Graham Greene; Caroline Ratski, Philip Mayer's daughter, who was helpful with the family's history; Bruce Hunter; Carey Winfrey; Elisabeth Buxton; and Greg Michalson for years of publishing advice.

A NOTE ABOUT THE AUTHOR

Michael Mewshaw's five-decade career includes award-winning fiction, nonfiction, literary criticism, travel writing, and investigative journalism. In his memoirs, Mewshaw has written about authors such as William Styron, James Jones, Paul Bowles, Anthony Burgess, Pat Conroy, Gore Vidal, and Italo Calvino. He has published hundreds of articles, reviews, and literary profiles in the *New York Times,* the *Washington Post,* the *Los Angeles Times, The Nation, Newsweek, Harper's,* and many other international outlets. Friends with Graham Greene for the last twenty years of Greene's life, Mewshaw's correspondence with the author is archived in its entirety at Boston College and the University of Texas.

A NOTE ON THE TYPE

My Man in Antibes has been set in Granjon. The typeface is named in honor of Robert Granjon, a bold French type-designer who, between 1557 and 1562, printed about twenty books in types designed by himself. Granjon was designed by George W. Jones in the late 1920s for the British branch of the Linotype company. The roman letters were inspired by the work of Claude Garamond, while the italics honor Granjon's passion for the cursive handwriting fashionable in the 1500s.

Design & Composition by Tammy Ackerman